SS-Charlemagne

The 33rd Waffen-Grenadier Division of the SS

Tony Le Tissier

Pen & Sword
MILITARY

First published in Great Britain in 2010
and reprinted in this format in 2019 by
Pen & Sword MILITARY
An imprint of Pen & Sword Books Ltd
Yorkshire – Philadelphia

Copyright © Tony Le Tissier, 2010, 2019
ISBN: 978 1 52675 662 6

Typeset in Ehrhardt by Phoenix Typesetting, Auldgirth, Dumfriesshire
Printed and bound in the UK by TJ International, Padstow, Cornwall

Pen & Sword Books Limited incorporates the imprints of Atlas, Archaeology,
Aviation, Discovery, Family History, Fiction, History, Maritime, Military, Military
Classics, Politics, Select, Transport, True Crime, Air World, Frontline Publishing, Leo
Cooper, Remember When, Seaforth Publishing, The Praetorian Press, Wharncliffe
Local History, Wharncliffe Transport, Wharncliffe True Crime and White Owl.

For a complete list of Pen & Sword titles please contact
PEN & SWORD BOOKS LIMITED
47 Church Street, Barnsley, South Yorkshire, S70 2AS, England
E-mail: enquiries@pen-and-sword.co.uk • Website: www.pen-and-sword.co.uk
Or
PEN AND SWORD BOOKS
1950 Lawrence Rd, Havertown, PA 19083, USA
E-mail: Uspen-and-sword@casematepublishers.com
Website: www.penandswordbooks.com

Contents

List of Maps

List of Plates

Preface

On VE Day, 8 May 1945, a firing squad from General Leclerk's 2nd Armoured Division summarily executed twelve prisoners from the Depot Battalion of the 33rd Waffen-Grenadier-Division of the SS-*Charlemagne* as traitors in a woodland clearing near the village of Karlstein in southeastern Bavaria. These prisoners had been part of a batch taken in the area by American troops and handed over to the Free French forces as they moved on.

If nothing else, this incident brought home the consequences of collaboration with the Germans during their occupation of France and the complications of interpreting and assessing such matters in relation to the prevailing political situation. The subject remains open for debate.

This book is mainly based upon material collated and most generously provided by Monsieur Robert Soulat, a former member of the *Charlemagne*, whose experience as a corporal clerk in the organisation provided the incentive. I was reluctant at first to undertake the task of writing up this story, as it involves such a complicated and sensitive era in French history, but in the end I could not let this interesting material go to waste.

In the spring of 1944 a new OKW general order foresaw the transfer of all foreign soldiers serving in the German Army to the Waffen-SS in order to simplify and improve their organisation. The assassination attempt against Hitler of 20 July 1944 accelerated this transfer, and particularly that of the French volunteers, who found themselves among the last involved in this reorganisation. Further, the two principal organisations concerned, the *Légion des*

Volontaires Français (LVF) and the French Storm Brigade of the Waffen-SS, were then both currently engaged on the Eastern Front, where the situation was becoming increasingly critical.

Under *Reichsführer-SS* Heinrich Himmler's pseudo-mystic leadership, the greatly expanded wartime Waffen-SS was considered to consist of three categories of personnel, German, Germanic and non-Germanic, the French fitting into the latter category. This classification was also reflected in formation titles, with 'volunteer' used in Germanic formation titles and non-Germanic titles being styled 'Waffen-Division der SS'. However, the title of 'Division' did not necessarily mean that it met that establishment in either numbers or equipment.

Though eventful, the life of the *Charlemagne* as a brigade, division and finally battalion from August 1944 to May 1945 was brief. Uniformed, equipped, trained and commanded as a Waffen-SS unit, its members were listed with SS ranks bearing the *Waffen* prefix, i.e. *W-Obersturmmführer* (lieutenant) as opposed to *SS-Obersturmführer*. I have therefore translated all ranks into their British equivalents and only used the SS prefix for German Waffen-SS personnel. Also, although the rank of *SS-Brigadeführer und Generalmajor der Waffen-SS* actually equated to Brigadier in the British Army, I have used SS-Major-General in my translation, to allow the insertion of the intermediate rank of *Oberführer*, peculiar to the Waffen-SS, as Brigadier.

We should be under no illusions as to what kind of people enlisted in or were compulsorily transferred into the *Charlemagne*. As we shall see, there may have been some honest political motivation among the original members of the *Légion des Volontaires Français* of 1941, but the *Miliciens* who swelled the ranks in 1944 were essentially fugitives from the wrath of their now mainly Gaullist or Communist compatriots, who considered them as both outcasts and renegades.

Nevertheless, it should be noted that no war crimes could later be attributed to the *Charlemagne*. It fought both bravely and well.

Chapter One

Formation

The crushing military defeat of France in 1940 arose out of many factors, but principally out of the devastating results of the First World War of 1914–1918, from which the country had yet to recover. The country's faith in the defences of the Maginot Line had been shattered when the German blitzkrieg smashed through between the French mobile forces covering the still open northern flank and the Maginot Line itself. Poor military leadership and lack of political willpower led to a swift disintegration of the state and humiliating surrender.

Following the signing of the armistice at Compiègne on the 22 June 1940, the new French government, headed by Marshal Henri Philippe Pétain with Pierre Laval as Deputy Premier, settled in the town of Vichy. France was now divided into occupied and unoccupied zones, but the coastal and border areas became restricted zones, while the provinces of Alsace and Lorraine were absorbed into the Third Reich, coming under the German conscription laws, as did the Duchy of Luxembourg, and the conscripts from these areas were deliberately deployed away from their home territory.

With the population stunned by the crushing defeat of French arms and the German invasion, Pétain and Laval sought to set aside the political turmoil of the inter-war years under the Third Republic by reviving morale with what they dubbed a National Revolution devoted to 'Work, Family and Country'.

On 11 October 1940, Pétain broadcast a speech to the nation in which he alluded to the possibility of France and Germany working together once peace had been established in Europe, using the word 'collaboration' in this context. In any case, with 1,700,000 French servicemen in German prisoner-of-war camps, his government had little alternative but to comply.

The Germans, on the other hand, were out to avenge their own humiliation at Versailles at the end of the previous war, and had no real interest in establishing a sympathetic ally or even an independent fascist state in France. In its relationship with France, all other concerns were subordinate to German interests.

A plethora of collaborationist political movements arose in the Paris area. The principal parties concerned were the Mouvement Social Révolutionaire (MSR), founded by Eugène Deloncle, Marcel Bucard's Parti Franciste, the Parti Populaire Français (PPF), founded in 1936 by Jacques Doriot, and the Rassemblement National Populaire (RNP), founded in February 1941 and led by Marcel Déat and Eugène Deloncle.

On 22 June 1941, the day that Adolf Hitler began his attack on the Soviet Union, Jacques Doriot launched the idea of forming a legion of French volunteers to fight Bolshevism alongside the German Army. The Germans were not particularly enthusiastic about allowing the French to participate, but eventually approval was given on 5 July 1941 for the formation of the *Légion des Volontaires Français* (LVF), limiting the effective strength to 100,000 men. It was to be recruited from men aged 18 to 45, born of Aryan parents and in good health.

Marshal Henri Philippe Pétain's Vichy Government supported this initiative, sending a telegram with his best wishes to the head of the LVF, and the Prefects of Departments also gave their support. Despite an impressive press campaign, only 1,600 volunteers came forward, out of which only 800 passed the strict German medical examinations, and were assembled at Versailles, where they held the first parade at the Borguis-Desbordes Barracks on 27 August 1941. The reasons for volunteering were mainly ideological, out of catholic or political conviction, but also because of the attractively high rates of pay and allowances. Between July 1941 and June 1944, some 13,000 volunteers were to apply, but only about half of these passed the rigorous German medical examinations.

Doriot left in September 1941 as an NCO with the first contingent of volunteers for Deba in Poland, where the recruits were equipped with German uniforms bearing a tricolour sleeve badge, and mustered into the Wehrmacht's *Infanterie-Regiment 638* under the command of 65-year-old Colonel Roger Henri Labonne (1881–1966), a former officer of French colonial troops. They were also required to swear an oath of allegiance to Adolf Hitler as commander-in-chief. Both the uniform and the oath came as a shock to the volunteers, who had been expecting to wear French uniforms and saw no reason for swearing the oath to a foreign commander-in-chief, but these obstacles were quickly overcome with the enthusiastic aid of their padre, the Roman Catholic, national socialist enthusiast, Monsignor de Mayol de Lupé. They would, however, be allowed to wear French uniforms when on leave in France.

The regiment consisting of two battalions, the 1st under Captain Leclercq, later Major de Planard, the 2nd under Major Girardeau, then left Deba at the end of October and reached Smolensk on 6 November 1941. No better equipped for the severity of the Russian winter than the rest of the German Army at that time, the troops then marched towards Moscow in blizzards and icy rain, their heavy equipment following them in horse-driven wagons. By the time they reached the front, only 63km from Moscow, a third of the men were suffering from dysentery and the regiment had lost 400 from sickness or straggling. The regiment was then assigned to the 7th Infantry Division and the regimental headquarters established in Golovkovo.

On 1 December, with the temperature down to -40 °C, the 1st Battalion was ordered to attack elements of the 32nd Siberian Division in a snowstorm. Within a week the 1st Battalion was so depleted that it had to be replaced by the 2nd Battalion. By 9 December, when the regiment was taken out of the line, it had suffered 65 killed, 120 wounded and over 300 cases of frostbite.

Lieutenant-Colonel Reichet, the divisional chief-of-staff reported: 'The men are keen enough, but lack military training. The NCOs are quite good, but cannot do much because of their inefficient superiors. The officers are incapable and were only recruited on political criteria. The Legion is not fit for combat. Improvement can only be achieved by renewal of the officer corps and thorough military training.'

The regiment was then sent back to Poland, where 1,500 volunteers were dismissed and returned to France, together with most of the officers, including Colonel Labonne. A fresh batch of volunteers arrived to replenish the ranks and training continued with an emphasis on the NCO backbone. The remains of the two existing battalions were merged and a new second battalion formed from fresh volunteers arriving from France. Eventually the regiment was reorganised into 3 battalions of about 900 men each, which were then allocated separately to various security divisions to assist in anti-partisan operations behind the lines, where the German assessment of the LVF remained poor. In February 1944, the regiment was reunited and assigned to the 286th Security Division.

On 18 July 1942, the Vichy Government instituted *La Légion Tricolore* as an official French Army replacement for the LVF, but the Germans refused to accept this concept and after only six months its members were absorbed into the LVF.

In June 1943, Colonel Edgar Puaud (1889–1945), a former officer in the French Foreign Legion, was given command of the LVF. Marshal Pétain later promoted him to the rank of general in the French Army, and made him a *Chevalier de la Legion d'Honneur*, but the Germans were not prepared to accept him in that rank, and he initially served with the rank of a Wehrmacht colonel.

Another 91 officers, 390 NCOs and 2,825 soldiers left for the Eastern Front in 1943, but incidents with the police involving LVF volunteers on leave did nothing to enhance their reputation. Militarily ineffective and supplied with recruits of dubious quality, the LVF remained a political and propaganda instrument of the collaborationist parties, despised by most Frenchmen, and considered suspect both politically and militarily by the Germans.

Consequent upon a new decree of 23 July 1943 enabling direct enlistment into the Waffen-SS, a new recruiting drive began in the Unoccupied Zone (Vichy France), attracting some 3,000 volunteers. This led to the formation of the *Französische SS-Freiwilligen Grenadier Regiment* (French SS-Volunteer Grenadier Regiment) the following month. Also known as the *Brigade Frankreich* or the *Brigade d'Assault des Volontaires Français*, it was placed under the command of the 18th SS-Panzer-Grenadier Division *Horst Wessel* in Galicia, where it suffered heavy casualties.

Parallel to the LVF, other Frenchmen were engaged in the German Army and Navy (Kriegsmarine), the NSKK (Nazi Party Transport Corps), whose units were gradually becoming armed, the Organisation *Todt* (OT) (Construction Corps), police and guard units. Individuals from these various organisations now began leaving to enlist in the Waffen-SS.

In fact, the creation of this first French SS unit signalled a deep change in the type of engagement. From then on the political aspirations of the collaborationist parties had little impact. It was no longer a question of fighting for the glory of France, but for Europe, primarily for a national-socialist German victory. As someone commented: 'The French SS are in fact purely and simply German soldiers.'

On 27 August 1943, the second anniversary of the founding of the LVF, a battalion of the regiment paraded at Les Invalides in Paris, where General Bridoux, the Vichy Minister of War, presented the regiment with a new Colour. This Colour, which was of the regular French Army pattern, bore the legend '*Honneur et Patrie*' and the battle honours '1941-1942 Djukowo' and '1942-1943 Bérésina'. There was then a presentation of awards to wounded veterans, and a march past in their honour by the mounted Garde Républicaine. Led by a company in German uniform and carrying their Tricolore standard, the battalion then marched to Notre Dame for a celebration of mass before proceeding up the Avenue des Champs Elysées for a wreath-laying ceremony at the Arc de Triomphe, cheered all the way by representatives of the many political parties supporting collaboration with the Germans.

The LVF was still an active force. As the German forces reeled back from the Soviet onslaught of 1944, Major Eugène Bridoux's battalion was called upon to form a combat team to block the Moscow–Minsk road in front of Borrisov near the Beresina River. On 22 June, his battalion, along with police units and a handful of tanks, fought a delaying action until the following evening that cost it 41 dead and 24 wounded, but inflicted considerable damage to the Soviets, including the loss of some 40 tanks. It fought so well that the Soviet opponents reported being up against two divisions. Exhausted and starving, the survivors reached the LVF depot at Greifenberg two weeks later. Here all French servicemen within the German armed forces were being assembled.

In the spring of 1944 the German High Command (OKW) had issued a general order foreseeing the transfer of all foreign soldiers serving in the German armed forces to the Waffen-SS in order to simplify the situation and maintain the strength of the Waffen-SS, for which German citizens were exempt from conscription by law and could only volunteer. The French were some of the last to be affected by this order, both the LVF and the French SS-Storm Brigade still being actively engaged on the Eastern Front.

The creation of the Waffen-SS *Charlemagne* Brigade was decided in August 1944 when *Reichsführer-SS* Heinrich Himmler gave the necessary orders for the LVF and the French SS-Storm Brigade to assemble during September at the Waffen-SS training area northeast of Konitz in the former Danzig Corridor. To these troops were added some 3,000–3,500 French volunteers from the German Navy, the latter coming via the LVF depot at Greifenberg in Pomerania, which was to become the *Charlemagne* Brigade depot. Individual transfers from Wehrmacht units were to continue to arrive right until the *Charlemagne* left for the front.

Once it had been assembled, the Brigade was moved to Wildflecken Camp in Franconia, 90km northeast of Frankfurt-am-Main and about 900m high in the Rhön massif, where the first companies detrained on 28 October, replacing elements of the SS-*Wallonien* and *Hitler-Jugend* Divisions.

Then, on 5 November, a reinforcement of 1,500 *Miliciens* arrived from France to be absorbed into the Brigade. They were not generally welcome. The *Milice Français* had been created by Premier Pierre Laval on 31 January 1943 as his own private police force, with Joseph Darnand as its Inspector General. Then on 2 June, the *Franc Garde* wing of the *Milice* was created for police and security tasks in the Unoccupied Zone under the command of Major Jean de Vaugelas, but remained unarmed until November, during which time several members were assassinated by members of the Resistance. Discussions with the SS led to an agreement whereby, in exchange for the provision of light weapons, the *Milice* would encourage enlistment in the Waffen-SS. Some 200 *Miliciens* then joined the Waffen-SS, including Henri Fenet, who was later to play a prominent role in the *Charlemagne*.

On 27 January 1944, the *Milice* was given permission to recruit in the Occupied Zone, and Jean Bassompierre and François Gaucher were recalled from the LVF on the Eastern Front to become inspectors in this organisation. The strength of the *Milice* rose in mid-1944 to 30,000, of which 10–12,000 were members of the *Franc Garde* active in the rounding up of Jews and assisting the German troops against the Resistance in what was virtually a civil war, gaining the *Miliciens* a reputation for assassination of political opponents, brutality and torture.

By August 1944, with Paris liberated and much of France under Allied control, the *Milice* and their families had to flee. Darnand led convoys of them, running the gauntlet to the relative security of Lorraine, where 6,000 *Miliciens* and 4,000 of their dependants gathered before moving on to Germany. Of these, 1,500 *Miliciens* opted to join the *Charlemagne*, while Darnand took most of the remainder to fight against the partisans in northern Italy. Those that did get through paid a heavy price: 76 were executed by firing squad in the Grand Bornand following a peremptory trial by their compatriots on 24 August. Consequently, the absorption of the *Miliciens* into the *Charlemagne* was not an easy matter, as we shall see.

The formation of the *Charlemagne* as a Waffen-SS unit was allocated to SS-Major-General Dr Gustav Krukenberg. Born on 8 March 1888 in Bonn, Krukenberg had ended the First World War as a young second-lieutenant attached to the General Headquarters at Spa with Kaiser Wilhelm II. Between the wars he lived more than five years in Paris, where he had formed several relationships in journalist and diplomatic circles, and came to understand the French mentality particularly well. From Paris he had moved to Berlin, where he worked as a legal adviser to an English firm in the chemical industry.

In 1939 Dr Krukenberg was mobilised in various headquarters in the rank of colonel of the reserve, his last position being with *Wirtschaftstab Ost*. He then spent time as chief-of-staff to the Vth SS-Mountain Corps in Yugoslavia. He was then transferred from the Army to the Waffen-SS as Inspector of SS Latvian formations and, after the invasion of Latvia by the Red Army in July 1944, he organised the defence of Dunaburg with these local forces with considerable success. On 24 September 1944, he was promoted to SS-*Brigadeführer und Generalmajor der Waffen-SS*, and assigned as Inspector of SS French formations.

In a memorandum prepared by him in 1958, Krukenberg recalled his tasks:

a) Put into effect and supervise all the measures ordered by
   the OKW guaranteeing the incorporation of the volunteers from various elements of the Wehrmacht [LVF, OT,
   Navy, NSKK, etc.].

b) Control of the aptitude of members of the Brigade – old and new – of all ranks to their engagement at the front and in the performance of their methods of combat. [Krukenberg was used to sacking incompetent NCOs and soldiers and in making the necessary demands in the case of officers.]

c) Examining the equipment and armament of the Brigade, as well as the organisation of the supply services, which, as for the LVF, remained a German responsibility. [A quartermaster was appointed as a result of this inspection.]

d) Supervising the theoretical and practical instruction of former French Army officers and NCOs to ensure that their tactical training and military habits conformed to German conceptions.

e) Establishing a military training plan for the troops and surveillance of its execution, despatching officers and soldiers to courses at various German military schools of the various arms.

f) Initiating and maintaining all measures to psychologically prepare those members of the Brigade who had not previously experienced defensive fighting against the Red Army.

g) Before the transfer to the front – and giving full command authority to the French commander of the Brigade – acting as intermediary with the German headquarters.

h) Taking into account all the directives, transforming the Brigade into a Division in the spring of 1945. [Without imposing on the French commander's position, the Inspector continued to act as the Division's supreme Judge Advocate General.]

i) Thanks to an organisation immediately subordinate to the Inspectorate, alleviating the concern of the French soldiers with regard to their families on German territory.

General Krukenberg then requested and obtained the approval of the High Command for the following points considered by him to be necessary:-

1) The line of conduct for French volunteers of all ranks could only be, in accordance with their terms of engagement, defensive fighting against the Soviet Army advancing on Western Europe.

2) Despite what Colonel Puaud had said, every volunteer had the right at the time of transferring to the Waffen-SS to terminate the terms of enlistment formerly entered into by him with other arms of the Wehrmacht. This was equally applicable to the new arrivals. Those who wanted to leave should be released without making it difficult for them. Nevertheless, they could only use this opportunity once.

3) To respect to a large extent the religious sentiments of the French volunteers, who almost without exception considered their engagements to be in defence of the Christian West, a point that had played a decisive role in their enrolment in France, and to support this point of view in the form of the divisional chaplain, Monsignor Comte de Mayol de Lupé and his auxiliaries.

4) There was no question of applying national-socialist propaganda among the volunteers. They were to remain French and not just French-speaking SS. The manner in which they saw the future of their country was their business. The troops were not to treat this matter otherwise than official. Arguments about internal political matters were to be discouraged as endangering the spirit of camaraderie.

5) The honour of the French flag and the prestige of the French soldier remained supreme not only in battle, but also in the way the German civilian population regarded them.

Krukenberg wrote of the arrival of the *Miliciens*:

In October 1944, the SS Main Office transferred several thousand [1,500] members of the *Milice Française* to the *Charlemagne* Division. They had retreated into southern Germany with their chief, Darnand, ahead of the advance of General de Gaulle's liberation forces. The latter (Darnand) remained in Sigmaringen, sending his followers to Wildflecken, where their arrival posed a problem for the already assembled volunteers, especially those from the Storm Brigade, who refused to accept them. This was particularly due to Darnand's activities as the Vichy Government's Chief of Police. They believed, not without reason, that the particular nature of the *Milice*'s employment in France would harm the reputation of other members of the Division in the eyes of their fellow countrymen. Apart from this, in their constituent formation the militiamen were an insecure factor for the whole Division. With the Inspector's [Krukenberg's] permission, they were divided up among all the units and their new oath taking ceremony ordered for [12] November.

Without being invited, Darnand wanted to come and watch this at Wildflecken. He arrived late and after the ceremony. He vividly criticised the fact that his men had not been kept in a specially separated unit and above all that we had not been satisfied with the initial oath [they had previously taken] to him personally. He expressed his two criticisms in a letter to SS-*Obergruppenführer* Berger, Chief of the SS Main Office, whom he considered his personal friend, firstly because they had fought against each other in the same sector during the First World War, and secondly because they had been in agreement over the actions conducted in occupied France. Darnand complained to the German Inspector – and also to the Laval Government – that 'he had been deprived of his last combatants.' On Himmler's orders, he was nevertheless obliged to retract his letter.

This did not prevent Darnand from appearing again soon – still without warning – at the Division, this time in the uniform of an SS-*Sturmbannführer* [Major] To the Inspector, who asked him if he wanted to demonstrate his membership and stay a while with the troops, he said that he had come charged with a mission from the French Government, of which he was a member with the rank of Secretary of State. He wanted to address the *Charlemagne*. The Inspector said that he was not competent to authorise such a step, and Darnard became very angry.

The senior French officer was still Colonel Puaud, who had expected to be appointed to the same rank as Krukenberg, but the Germans did not want to have a French SS-General among their ranks, and only accorded him the rank of SS-*Oberführer* (Brigadier). However, in an interview with *Reichsführer-SS* Heinrich Himmler at the SS Main office in Berlin, Puaud was given the following assurances:

1. The Brigade would fight under the French flag.
2. One would avoid, as far as possible, engaging it on a front where it would find itself exposed to fighting other Frenchmen.
3. Although the Brigade was an SS unit, the practice of Christian religions in it would be absolutely free of restraint.
4. Finally, the capital point, in case of a German victory, the integrity of French national territory and its colonies would be scrupulously guaranteed.

The Vichy Government had been compulsorily removed to the German town of Sigmaringen on the Danube in August, causing both Marshal Pétain and Laval to refuse to continue to function in their roles. However, they had appointed Fernand de Brinon, who had been Vichy's official Delegate in the Occupied Zone, to exercise his authority on behalf of the French citizens on German soil (POWs and workers) as head of the so-called French Governmental Delegation in Sigmaringen.

Krukenberg suspected that the French Governmental Delegation was considering fielding the *Charlemagne* on the Western Front, which would have been totally against the volunteers' terms of enlistment. Krukenberg later wrote of Puaud that:

> . . . when he was nominated commander of the *Charlemagne* in September 1944, the latter had told the OKW in the name of both units that their volunteers agreed to their transfer to the new Division. It was impossible to verify to what extent he was justified in making such a declaration. In any case, on the day of arrival of the newly appointed Inspector, a certain number of volunteers opposed the transfer, upon which Puaud, without authority and without the knowledge of the new Inspector (Krukenberg), sent the opponents to a concentration camp. Next day the Inspector had them brought back by his intelligence officer and demobilised them.

The OKW had forbidden the Inspector all contact with Sigmaringen. Should the need arise, contact would be conducted in either direction by the OKW. The SS Main Office alone remained competent on all questions of enrolment or assignment of volunteers and for all units formed from foreigners.

The unification of the various comprising units gave rise to much debate and friction as a consequence of the different aims of the volunteers in each of these units from the outset. The opposing views of the various political parties were fortunately more artificial than realistic and all these volunteers were agreed on the absolute necessity of the fight against Bolshevism.

The principal component remained the LVF, which had the distinction of having been first in battle. Purged by its long campaign in Russia, it no longer contained any of the doubtful elements or *arrivistes* of 1941–1942. The LVF, despite its revised appellation as Wehrmacht *Grenadier-Regiment 638*, regarded itself with pride as an exclusively French unit, part of the French Army, commanded in French by French officers under the French flag, representing France on the Russian Front according to the instructions of the legitimate head of the French state, Marshal Pétain.

As for Germany, it was for them their neighbour, and it is always best to get on well with one's neighbours. In the face of a common danger, one must stand shoulder to shoulder, and since Germany found itself suddenly the sword and buckler of Europe against Bolshevism, it was natural to fight shoulder to shoulder with its soldiers. Should there be a German victory, France's interests would have a say in the matter, and the LVF provided this possibility.

Many of the legionaries, some of whom had once been militants in the Communist Party and had followed Jacques Doriot when he broke away from it, agreed that it was preferable to take up the anti-Bolshevik fight openly as a soldier on the Russian steppes rather than on French territory against other Frenchmen, most of whom were as mistaken in their views as they themselves had been.

The remnants of the LVF and the SS-Sturmbrigade provided about 1,200 men each for the *Charlemagne*.

The *Miliciens* similarly regarded themselves as belonging to the National Revolution and loyal to the Marshal, but reproached the *legionaires* for having adopted German uniform and for deserting their primary duty to France. By this they meant directly combating those terrorists and guerrillas operating under communist direction in France, a task they primarily regarded as an interior matter to be settled among Frenchmen, and not one to be left to the German army of occupation.

On the subject of Franco-German relations, the *Miliciens* were animated by the same sentiments as the members of the LVF and their patriotism was certainly no less. At the same time it was their political origin that led them to regard the fight on French soil against the communist-led *Francs-Tireurs et Partisans* as far more important than that against the guerrillas of the Secret Army (*l'Armée Secréte*).

They did not have to be told of the importance of the fight on the Eastern Front and it should be noted that the original French members of the Waffen-SS were former *Miliciens*, a point that many members of the *Charlemagne* Brigade forgot when accusing them of being latecomers!

The 1,500 volunteers coming from the German Navy had little in common with the others save taking orders in German. For the rest, they were far less idealistic than any in the other formations.

There were also about 1,000 volunteers each from the NSKK (National Socialist Transportation Corps) and the Organisation *Todt* construction corps.

The invasion of France by the Western Allies dried up the source of new volunteers, condemning the various units already in existence to a more or less rapid but certain thinning out. But a major French formation was to remain on the anti-Bolshevist front right until the end of the conflict.

The French Waffen-SS was to produce a new type of combatant, young and fanatical, most of whom, not having served in any other army, could be typified as the 'European Soldier'. They were like brothers to the other European soldiers of the Waffen-SS. They were no longer just Frenchmen, as the others were no longer just Danes, Letts, Germans or Belgians. More amenable than the older men to German military instruction, they were commanded in German, manoeuvred in German and sang in German, all things appearing somewhat scandalous to the Brigade's original volunteers, but was this not the common language of the Axis forces in the European Army? Their symbol was no longer the Tricolore or the war flag with the swastika of the Greater German Reich, but the black flag with white runes of the Waffen-SS.

The founding of a large combat-ready unit with this variety of components posed some difficult problems for SS-Major-General

Krukenberg and *Waffen-Oberführer* Puaud to resolve. But the fusion of these elements under the Waffen-SS cloak, which was at that time the subject of an incredible number of reservations, scruples or criticisms by the parties concerned, appears to have been the only practical and sustainable solution. In 1944 the Waffen-SS was, much more than the strictly German Wehrmacht, the true upholder of the European concept, and the only place for non-German Eurpeans was in its ranks.

Krukenberg was fortunate to have SS-*Standartenführer* (Colonel) Walter Zimmermann as the officer responsible for training. Born on 1 October 1897 at Meissen in Saxony, and a former member of the 'Black Reichswehr', Zimmermann had joined the new Wehrmacht in 1935, from where he transferred to an engineer battalion of the Waffen-SS at Dresden. He too had been attached to the Vth SS-Mountain Corps, in which he had served as Chief of Engineers. He soon became the most popular of the German officers through his tact and knowledge of Parisian slang. His capacities were stretched even further and he was to prove himself in Pomerania.

The Inspectorate headquarters, completely German, supervised the Brigade's headquarters, which was entirely French, until it became the Divisional headquarters at the front in February 1945.

At first the Brigade at Wildflecken was commanded as follows:

Brigade: *W-Oberführer* (Brigadier) Puaud (LVF)
57th Regt: Major Gamory-Dubourdeau (SS)
58th Regt: Major Bridoux (LVF)
Heavy Bn: Captain de Vaugelas (*Milice*)

Soon after their arrival at Wildflecken, as a result of their French Army qualifications the senior *Milice Française* officers obtained the main command posts within the Brigade. There was considerable upheaval among the officers at this stage, and during February 1945. A total of fifteen officers, including Lieutenant

Coutray, a friend of Darnard, were returned to France for various reasons.

To everyone's surprise Major Bridoux suddenly resigned and left the Brigade at the beginning of December 1944 following a visit by his father, General Bridoux, the Vichy Minister of War. Before leaving, he tried to encourage other officers to follow his example. His departure suited Brigadier Puaud, who saw him as a potential rival for command of the *Charlemagne*, and tried to camouflage Major Bridoux's departure as leave. Indeed, some of the Waffen-SS liaison staff would have liked to have seen Bridoux in command. His upright character had not only made him many friends, but he was held in high esteem by the Germans, to whom he would recite extracts from Hindenburg's memoirs.

Then Major Paul-Marie Gamory Dubourdeau, a former lieu-tenant-colonel in the French Army, was posted to the SS Main Office to head the French Department under SS-General Berger, and the two vacant regimental commands were taken over by Captains Victor de Bourmont and Emile Raybaud.

De Bourmont, a captain serving with the *Tirailleurs Algériens*, a prisoner of war released after volunteering for service in Syria, but too late for action, had then commanded the *Milice* in Lyon. Straightforward, reasonable and well-loved by his men, he was given command of the 57th Regiment of former SS men but, in contrast to de Vaugelas, Raybaud and Boudet-Gheusi, was not promoted Major until going to the front.

Raybaud, born in 1910, formerly an officer with the *Chasseurs Alpins*, who had served with the *Milice* at Limousin, a particularly devoted and courageous officer, was given command of the 58th Regiment of former LVF personnel.

Captain Jean de Vaugelas, born in 1915, a French Air Force captain in 1940, commander of the 2nd Cohort of the *Milice* at Glières in the Limousin, became Brigade chief-of-staff.

Captain Monneuse, former chief of the 5th Cohort of the *Milice* at Dijon, a 50-year-old of little military appearance, but patriotic, honest and courageous and with a good military grounding, was given command of the 1st Battalion of the 58th.

Then the *Milice* officers Captain de Bourmont and Bassompierre (an earlier transfer from the LVF to the *Milice*) were sent on a battalion commanders' course. In all the *Miliciens* received a good number of command posts, in particular that of Captain de Vaugelas as chief-of-staff to the Brigade.

During the harsh winter of 1944–1945, while the grenadiers trained under the difficult conditions imposed by the cold, snow, sparse rations and lack of clothing and equipment, the future specialists were trained at the Waffen-SS special military schools.

The *Charlemagne* sent two batches of candidates to the officer-cadet school at Neweklau. Some thirty potential officers, mainly LVF, went from Saalesch, while others went direct from their officers' prisoner-of-war camp. The course lasted three terms, and concentrated on the training of leaders and directing small units on exercise as *Panzergrenadiers*, using captured Russian T–34 tanks to work with. It also focused on the training of platoon and even company commanders and dealing with tactical problems.

Then in December 1944, a group mainly consisting of former *Miliciens* plus some former LVF that had already attended the first part of the course either at Deba or at Greifenberg attended just the second part of the Neweklau course. Several old firebrands from the LVF like Walter, Vincenot and Bellanger joined this course voluntarily, not wanting to go back to basic training after two or three years combat experience in Russia. Several of these individuals were to lead companies in Pomerania.

Selected candidates then took an examination at the end of six months. Elimination of unsuitable candidates took place particularly during the second term, and the 200 that had started in December were reduced to 50 by the end of March. 'Returns to unit' took place every fortnight, those concerned retaining their ranks and even being eligible for promotion to higher non-commissioned rank.

Conditions at the school were tough, to say the least. Few armies would have subjected their officer-cadets to such rough conditions. There was no heating in the abandoned Czech village, so one was entitled to flap one's arms once every half hour to warm up. For lack of hot water, the cadets shaved themselves with their morning coffee. They were always hungry, and in order to study at night in their rooms, they had to fashion candles out of boot polish.

Vigour, authority and responsibility were the order of the day. The instructors repeated: 'You can leave when you want; the door is open. We are not holding back anybody!' And it was true. 'We always had the choice,' wrote one of the candidates, 'but they were even more demanding once we had decided to continue.'

The candidates were woken up for exercises up to four times a night, and weapon handling took place in temperatures of -15 and -20 °C. But in this selection of an elite, the instructors never had to resort to bullying. Having made an assessment of the fighting on all the fronts, they said: 'Now it is clear that the war is technically lost, but we continue to be confident. Those who want to go can leave!'

The course finished at the end of March 1945. Some twenty to thirty Frenchmen were classified for promotion to second-lieutenant, but continued to wear the rank badges of officer-cadets, presumably remaining under probation. However, they were unable to rejoin the Division immediately and were first distributed among various units of the Regiment remaining behind, bringing them fresh blood. For three weeks their task was to bolster up the spirits of the young grenadiers demoralised by the fighting in Pomerania. They succeeded marvellously and without them the fighting in Berlin, where many of them were later to fall, would not have been possible.

The school was finally disbanded on 9 April and, apart from a small number sent to the depot at Wildflecken, the students returned to the units in Mecklenburg, where they arrived on 14th.

Meanwhile, those detailed for the specialist tasks within the division were dispersed to courses run at Josefstadt for gunners, Lissa for infantry gunners, Brunschau for engineers, Janowitz-Beneschau for anti-tank and self-propelled gun crews, Sterzing (Viptino) for signallers, Göttingen for mounted troops, Stettin for medical-aid men, Berlin for vehicle mechanics, Oranienburg for interpreters and Breslau for clerks. The last course at Breslau for company-quartermaster-sergeants was unfortunate, as the city was cut off by the Soviets while they were still undergoing their training and they were obliged to take part in the defence.

The Brigade's only fully trained unit was the flak battery, which had been transferred intact from the SS-French Storm Brigade and was sent off on 3 January 1945 to deploy in defence of the little town of Fulda, a frequent target for Anglo-American air raids. This unit of about 150 men had been designated the Storm Brigade's Flak Battery and was placed under the command of Captain Maudhuit, a veteran of the First World War, at Neweklau in Czechoslovakia. It contained several other former French Army officers in the current rank of sergeant-major, including Croisille, Crespin, Roy, the Count Foulques de Larentie and the Marquis de Tolosan, a former air attaché in Brussels.

Fayard, an officer-cadet fresh from the Bad Tölz SS School, was then attached to Captain Maudhuit and took over the training. Then Maudhuit was transferred and Sergeant-Major Guignot, a former captain in the Foreign Legion, took over the battery.

However, there were no proper facilities at Neweklau for training the battery, so on 25 April 1944, the unit entrained for Munich, where it was accommodated in the ultra-modern barracks of the SS-*Das Reich* Panzer Division. Three days later it received its official title as the *SS-Französische Flak-Batterie*, the only French unit to bear the title of SS, as opposed to *Waffen*.

Paradoxically, the 3rd Company that provided the Flak nucleus was a kind of disciplinary unit containing the hotheads whose behaviour while on leave in France had led to complaints to the German Military Administration.

At Munich it conducted its training alongside German troops, while the three platoon commanders, Fayard, who was to replace Guignot in the August, Ouvre and Mary attended a platoon commanders' course elsewhere. The battery also took an active and successful part in the defence of the city and their own barracks against the Anglo-American bombers.

After three month's training, on 28 July, the battery was issued with new uniforms and entrained for Bruss in the Danzig Corridor, where it was issued with its complete establishment of nine 37mm guns, arms, ammunition and vehicles. It then moved to Saalesch, and Officer-Cadet Fayard, soon to be promoted to second-lieutenant, took over the battery, which began training up to 10 hours a day.

Then, on 31 October, the battery entrained for Wildflecken Camp to join the *Charlemagne* Brigade. Some two months later, on 3 January 1945, being considered the only unit of the Brigade fit for combat, the Flak Battery was detached in defence of the little town of Fulda, a frequent target of Anglo-American air raids.

With the Greifenberg Depot under the command of Swiss SS-Major Hersche coming under threat from the Russian advance, it was obliged to move to Wildflecken. The Depot units consisted of the 1st Training Company under SS-Second-Lieutenant Schüler, the Depot Company under SS-Lieutenant Allgeier and the Recruit Company under Lieutenant Crespin. Having dispensed with about 250 undesirable or dubious characters, the Depot now amounted to about 400 men.

According to one of the instructors, the value of those elements trained at Greinfenberg was very mediocre. They were good at drill, but were not much use on the ground, not knowing how to conceal themselves or to spread out, and they also lacked firing training.

On 23 January 1945, all these depot elements were formed into a field replacement battalion under Captain Michel Bisiau, which eventually arrived to reinforce the Division at Körlin on 3 March.

The final establishment of the *Charlemagne* Division was as follows:

SS-Grenadier Regiment 57 of two battalions
   (continuing the SS connection)

SS-Grenadier Regiment 58 of two battalions
   (continuing the LVF connection)

SS-Artillery Regiment 57
   (one HQ and two gun batteries)

SS-Tank Hunting Battalion 57
   (combining tank destroyers, flak and armoured vehicles)

Divisional Units
   (engineers, signals, supply, etc. with the serial number
57):

Each regiment consisted of:

   HQ Company with:-
      HQ Staff
      – Reconnaissance Platoon
      – Pioneer Platoon
      – Signals Platoon
   3 x Rifle Companies, each of 144 men:-
         – HQ Platoon
         – 3 x Rifle Platoons (each of 3 sections)
         – 1 Heavy Machine Gun Section
   Tank Hunting Company:-
      – 50mm Pak Platoon
      – Panzerschreck Platoon
      – Panzerfaust Platoon
   Infantry Gun Company:-
      – HQ Platoon
      – Heavy Platoon (2 x 150mm guns)

- 3 x Light Platoons (each of 2 x 75mm guns (short-barrelled))
3 x Rifle Companies, each of 144 men and:-
- HQ Platoon
- 3 x Rifle Platoons (each of 3 sections)
- 1 Heavy Machine Gun Section
Heavy Weapons Company of 170 men:-
- HQ Platoon
- 2 x Mortar Platoons (4 x 80mm each)
- 3 x Heavy Machine Gun Platoons (4 x HMG each)
The Tank Hunting Battalion consisted of:-
- 1 x Heavy Company (75mm Pak)
- 1 x Flak Company (9 x 37mm)
- 1 x Assault Gun Company
- 1 x Infantry Escort Company
Each of the Artillery Regiment's batteries had 4 x 105mm guns.

Theoretically, the Brigade's fire-power was quite considerable, but in fact it was to be sent into action without its artillery and armoured vehicles, being thus deprived of 12 x 105mm pieces and 14 light tank-hunting Czech-built *Hetzer* tanks with 75mm guns.

The troop establishment was satisfactory, but that of the battalion and regimental headquarters less so, because of the lack of sufficient qualified technical personnel. There was a dearth of officers and, upon departure for the front, each of the regiments was only commanded by a captain, several companies by a WO I or II, and several platoons by a sergeant. The *Charlemagne*, now officially rated as a Division, consisted of 102 officers, 886 non-commissioned officers and 5,375 men, a total strength of 6,363 all ranks.

The command structures of the Inspectorate, Brigade, Regiments and Battalions with the names of the officers concerned prior to departure is given at Annex B.

Chapter Two

Action

The circumstances in which the *Charlemagne* was committed to war were indeed desperate.

In mid-January the Soviets had broken out of their bridgeheads across the Vistula River and swept up to the Oder River opposite Berlin by the end of the month in a lightening operation. But, in doing so the Soviets had left Pomerania out of the line of advance, enabling the Germans to muster a force there that was intended to strike south into the flank of the Soviet vanguards and annihilate them while Soviet lines of communication were still hampered by lack of bridges across the Vistula.

Under the prevailing conditions, with the old men of the Volkssturm and the 14-year-olds of the Hitler Youth being mobilised for defence, it was obvious that the departure of the *Charlemagne* for the front, even if insufficiently trained and equipped, could not be delayed much longer. Consequently, on 17 February 1945, the first elements of the *Charlemagne*, now officially up-graded to a division, entrained at Wildflecken railway station.

According to the orders received, upon arrival in the forward area the advance elements of the *Charlemagne* would report to Headquarters Army Group Weichsel. This Army Group had been created on 23 January from the wreckage of the 9th Army pushed back to the line of the Oder River by Marshal Zhukov's 1st Byelorussian Front, and the remains of the 2nd Army now standing with its back to the Baltic around Danzig as a result of the advance of Marshal Rokossovsky's 2nd Byelorussian Front. The commander of this new formation was *Reichsführer-SS* Heinrich

Himmler, who would later establish his headquarters at Prenzlau.

Incredibly, Himmler had arrived to take up this appointment in his personal train with only one *Waffen-SS* staff officer and a single map. His train then parked in Deutsch Eylau railway station, blocking the line for refugee trains heading west, and forbidding further evacuation of the civilian population, not that this order would be obeyed.

With the arrival of Himmler as commander of Army Group *Weichsel* came a plethora of police officers to keep order in the rear areas and, in particular, round up deserters and stragglers to return them to the front in march companies.

By this stage of the war, it was not uncommon for units to raid trains destined for other units in order make up their own deficiencies. With a view to preventing this, Himmler renewed his orders of 4 February in a telex of the 26th to SS-General Hans Juttner, who was standing in for him as commander of the Replacement Army, to ensure that every train carrying ammunition, fuel, vehicles or weapons destined for the front were to be escorted under command of an energetic officer of at least the rank of captain, assigned by name and personally responsible, to ensure that the wagons were not stolen, uncoupled, left in sidings or sent off in the wrong direction. This unusual state of affairs, which had become quite normal, despite the Wehrmacht's usual strict discipline, was to have grave consequences for the *Charlemagne*. Because of a serious situation arising in one of the areas through which it had to pass, either in Bohemia or Silesia, another formation appropriated all the *Charlemagne*'s *Hetzers* for its own more urgent needs.

It so happened that the Soviet had made a serious error in their planning, so that between Marshal Zhukov's thrust towards Berlin and Marshal Rokossovsky's thrust on Danzig, no allowance had been made for a simultaneous clearing of Pomerania, and it was into this gap, between the 9th Army lining the Oder and the 2nd Army defending Danzig–Gotenhafen area, that the German High Command began pouring a miscellany of hastily assembled units now assigned to SS-General Felix Steiner's 11th SS-Panzer Army. Then, taking advantage of this temporarily advantageous situation, Colonel-General Heinz Guderian, chief of the general staff, proposed a pincer movement to cut into Marshal Zhukov's forces from north and south, converging on Küstrin. Hitler, however, was more concerned with the situation in Hungary, to where he sent the bulk of his remaining armoured forces, leaving Guderian only the resources of the 11th SS-Panzer Army to mount Operation *Sonnenwende* (Solstice) for a thrust southwards into Zhukov's northern flank.

Guderian, concerned at Himmler's military ineptitude, after a long and blistering argument with Hitler, finally obtained agreement for the operation to be commanded by his own deputy, Lieutenant-General Walter Wenck. Operation *Sonnenwende* was launched on 15 February, achieving temporary surprise with a thrust by the 11th SS-*Nordland* Division on Arnswalde, where the besieged German garrison was relieved. The remaining German forces attacked on the 16th and also achieved some limited success over the next two days despite persistent Soviet counterattacks and also coming up against strong anti-tank defences of guns and mines.

On the 17th Wenck was summoned to Berlin to brief Hitler on the progress of the operation. On the way back Wenck took over the wheel from his exhausted driver, only to fall asleep himself and crash the car, hurting himself badly. General of Infantry Hans Krebs assumed control of the operation the next day, but by then the initiative had been lost. The German units had all been forced to go on the defensive and that evening Army Group *Weichsel* abandoned the attack. Some of the armoured elements were then immediately sent in haste to the Küstrin front, where the situation was even more critical, and SS-General Steiner was left with insufficient troops to continue.

In turn, Zhukov decided to launch an attack toward Stettin on 19 February, using the 2nd Guards Tank Army, the 61st Army and the 7th Guards Cavalry Corps. Two corps of the 61st Army surrounded

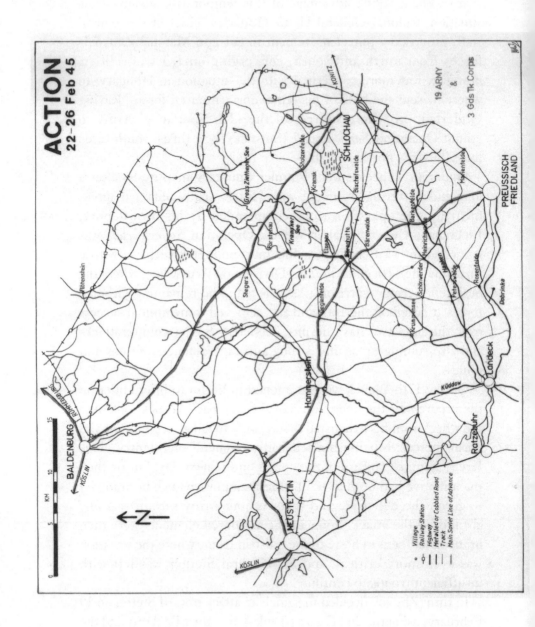

ACTION
22–26 Feb 45

RÜMHERSBURG

KÖSLIN

BALDENBURG

N

KM
0 5 10 15

Rötenstein

Gross Zietheh'n See

Stolzenfelde

KONITZ

Kranok

SCHLOCHAU

Bischofswalde

Für stenau

Kreuzsfan
See

Eisenau

Eisenhütte

Bärenwalde

Barkopfelde

Marienfelde

PREUSSISCH
FRIEDLAND

Sieges

Teglamfelde

Hammerstein

Schönwerder

Heinrichsau

Heinen

Petershtage

Rosenfelde

Krumpensee

Dobrinke

Landeck

Küddow

KÖSLIN

NEUSTETTIN

Ratzebuhr

19 ARMY
&
3 Gds Tk Corps

○ Village
⊖ Railway Station
│ Highway
║ Metalled or Cobbled Road
│ Track
│ │ Main Soviet Line of Advance

Arnswalde while one division went in to clear the town in bitter street fighting, so Zhukov temporarily called off the operation and switched to the defensive.

22 February 1945
The first trainload of the *Charlemagne* arrived at Hammerstein station on the Pomeranian boundary with East Prussia at 0200 hours on 22 February. This was unexpected, for when the train carrying the Divisional Headquarters had stopped at Gollnow, near Stettin, at about 1700 hours the previous day, Brigadier Puaud, SS-Colonel Zimmermann, Captain Renault and Officer-Cadet Platon had left the train and driven on to Rummelsburg, only to discover upon arrival that the train carrying the main body had meanwhile been diverted to Hammerstein. Now allocated to the 11th SS-Panzer Army, the Division was to regroup at Hammerstein Camp, where it would receive additional arms and equipment and have a week to prepare before going into the line.

However, back in Moscow after the distractions of the Yalta Conference, between 17 and 22 February the Soviet High Command issued fresh instructions to Marshals Zhukov and Rokossovsky calling for a combined attack that would split the Pomeranian group of German forces in half and then fan out to clear the area. In pursuance of these instructions, Rokossovsky launched his 2nd Byelorussian Front in an attack on 24 February in which the 3rd Guards Tank Corps and 19th Army spearheaded a northerly thrust to the Baltic coast near Köslin, while the main body did a right hook toward Danzig and Gotenhafen.

It was calculated that the German forces defending Pomerania were facing an enemy superiority of 1 to 3–5 in infantry, 1 to 2–4 in tanks and 1 to 4–6 in artillery.

24 February 1945
At Hammerstein Camp at dawn on 24 February, a strong artillery bombardment could be heard and seen some 15km to the south-east as the Soviets conducted an artillery preparation. Five

divisions of the Soviet 19th Army had launched an attack on the 32nd Infantry Division between Marienfelde and Konitz.

That same morning Major Emile Raybaud arrived by train with the 58th Regiment's headquarters and Captain Emile Monneuse's 1st Battalion.

Consequent upon the Soviet attack, the *Charlemagne* was now assigned to the 2nd Army's XVIIIth Mountain Corps, commanded by Lieutenant-General Hans Hochbaum. Until the arrival of the *Charlemagne*, this corps, which had no mountain troops, consisted of only the 32nd Infantry Division and the 15th Waffen-SS-Grenadier Division of Latvians, and was responsible for a 45km front, for which the *Charlemagne* came as a welcome reinforcement. The Latvians had their divisional headquarters in the village of Krummensee, with their two regiments covering the western flank along the Kuddow River through the town of Landeck and then facing southwards along the line of the Dobrinka River as far as the village of Rosenfelde. The 32nd Infantry had their headquarters at Stolzenfelde, north of Schlochau, and covered the line eastwards, north of Preussisch Friedland to Konitz.

Both divisions were of excellent fighting quality, the Latvians seeking revenge for the Russian invasion of their country, while the 32nd Infantry had been raised in Pomerania and was literally defending its home ground, but both had already been engaged with the enemy for a month and had suffered severe casualties.

During the course of the morning, a conference was held at the camp with SS-Major-General Krukenberg, Brigadier Puaud and the two regimental commanders, Captains Raybaud and Victor de Bourmont, attending. The front held by the Latvians had been penetrated and the Division had just received orders to plug the breach. The command intention was to form a stop line facing east in the area between Hammerstein and Schlochau, with the front supported by the Haaken River in the south and southwest and by the Kramsker See and Gross Ziethener See lakes in the north.

With only three battalions available, the orders for the move were given out immediately and took place at about midday as follows:

a) The 1st/57th (Lieutenant Henri Fenet) towards Heinrichswalde and Barkenfelde.
b) The 2nd/57th and HQ 57th Regt (Captain de Bourmont) towards Geglenfelde. (For tactical reasons the 57th Regiment was provisionally attached to the 32nd Infantry Division and was to hold the prescribed line of the front for about 7km running from south of Heinrichswalde to east of Barkenfelde. The right wing of the 32nd Infantry Division extended as far as Bärenhütte railway station.)
c) The 1st/58th (Captain Emile Monneuse) and HQ 58th Regt (Captain Emile Raybaud) to Bärenhütte as the divisional reserve.

However, it should be noted that not only was the Division incomplete, but it was going into action with only those items, including ammunition, that it had brought with it. There were no radios and only a few maps. The military installation at Hammerstein was empty of all military stores as a result of its previous use as a prisoner-of-war camp.

Fenet's 1st/57th left its temporary position and advanced towards Heinrichswalde, which it was to occupy and defend as a firm base of operations, but its march was delayed by the very poor state of the road. At times the carts carrying their heavy weapons and ammunition sank up to their hubs in the mud through which the troops had to march, while refugees fleeing in the opposite direction forced them to the side of the road. On the way Lieutenant Fenet learned that the Russians had broken through and were also heading for Heinrichswalde. The battalion immediately prepared to encounter the enemy.

Towards 1900 hours, as night fell, Second-Lieutenant Counil's leading 3rd Company was approaching Heinrichswalde when it was met by a hail of fire. The enemy had just occupied the village without a fight, for the front in this sector appeared to have been completely abandoned. Second-Lieutenant Counil estimated the enemy effectives no more than a company, so Lieutenant Fenet decided to attack in strength.

The 3rd Company would pin down the enemy from the southwest, the 1st Company would surround the village from the southeast and Lieutenant Bartholomei's 2nd Company from the northwest. During the mortar preparation by Staff-Sergeant Couvreur's 4th Company, the 2nd Company was to establish contact with the 2nd Battalion on the left, but none of the patrols sent out were able to make contact with anyone in that direction. The mortar preparation proved of short duration, as the ammunition soon ran out.

The 1st and 3rd Companies attacked, while the 2nd Company swept the ground to the east with automatic weapons, reducing the enemy resistance in the village. But the enemy machine guns proved judiciously well placed and the enemy effectives were now estimated at being a battalion. Flares and a clear night prevented further progress.

The 3rd Company advanced at the cost of very heavy losses, Second-Lieutenant Counil being killed, and rapidly reached the centre of the village, which it occupied and began to clear. When the 1st Company tried to advance, it was quickly checked by violent fire coming from heavy weapons. There was some hesitation, and a tentative flanking movement had no more success than the direct attack. The 2nd Company could not move, as enemy fire had it pinned down and the enemy could not be dislodged from this part of the village.

At this moment, the Soviets launched a violent counterattack to retake the village. The 3rd Company, reinforced by Battalion HQ, and supported by the fire of the other companies, intervened and neatly stopped the Russians, who resumed their attack several times, being rebuffed each time. Eventually Lieutenant Fenet was thinking of surrounding Heinrichswalde left and right with his 1st and 2nd Companies in a concentric attack, when the 1st Company signalled that Russians were advancing northwards unopposed between the Schönwerder and Peterswalde roads. The 2nd Company also reported that strong Russian infantry formations were advancing non-stop on Barkenfelde.

Towards midnight the Russians conducted a reconnaissance in strength with an infantry company reinforced by anti-tank guns and mortars advancing towards the 6th Company. The company commander, Second-Lieutenant Brunet, allowed the enemy to approach to within 20m of his positions before opening a murderous fire to cut down the attackers. The survivors avoided coming to close-quarter fighting and fled, but a little later a terrible bombardment fell on the battalion's positions for about an hour from Soviet artillery, 80mm and 120mm mortars, 76mm anti-tank guns and *Stalin Organ* rockets.

However, the two wings of Fenet's 1st/57th were now in the air, already bypassed, with no chance of liaison to either left or right, and about to be surrounded.

Meanwhile, things had not gone well in the 2nd/57th's sector. HQ 57 Regiment and Captain René-André Obitz's 2nd Battalion had arrived at Geglenfelde from Hammerstein at about noon. Learning that the Russians had already occupied the village of Barkenfelde, where he was supposed to have set up his command post, Captain de Bourmont immediately took up fighting positions with his regimental staff. The 32nd Infantry Division holding this sector had been so seriously crushed that there was no one left between them and the enemy.

Captain Obitz's 2nd/57th continued its advance to contact, while the regimental command post was being established in Bärenwalde. At about 1500 hours Second-Lieutenant Erdozain's Reconnaissance Section came into contact with an enemy detachment wearing German uniforms (turncoat German prisoners of war, so-called Seydlitz-Troops) several hundred metres from Bärenwalde, but managed to get away. The 2nd/57th immediately attacked from the march, threw back the enemy and reoccupied the village, which it held until the evening when, under pressure from fresh Soviet troops engaging against the French positions with a strength of about 10 to 1, Captain Obitz ordered the disengagement and retirement to a line of craters in front of Bärenwalde to the northeast of the road to Barkenfelde.

At about 1900 hours, things calmed down and reinforcements arrived. These were Lieutenant Serge Krotoff's heavy anti-tank company from the tank-hunting battalion, a battery of 105mm howitzers, and two 88mm flak guns detached from the 32nd Division.

Major Raybaud set up the 58th Regiment's command post in Bärenhütte during the afternoon, while Captain Monneuse's 1st/58th deployed on the other side of the road to Barkenfelde, where he organised his fighting positions on the southern edge of the Bärenwalde woods.

The bulk of the 58th Regiment having meanwhile arrived on foot, a conference was held in the 57th Regiment's command post attended by Major de Vaugelas (the Brigade chief-of-staff), SS-Captain Jauss (the Inspection's operations officer) and Captain Monneuse. The practical conclusion was that the 1st/58th should re-establish a continuous front between the 1st and 2nd Battalions of the 57th Regiment, which were isolated from each other, and to this end come under the command of the 57th Regiment as reinforcements. Brigadier Puaud at the Brigade HQ in Bärenwalde confirmed this order with Major Raybaud and also detached Lieutenant Michel Saint Magne's 6th Company of the 58th Regiment to a point halfway between Bärenhütte and Elsenau.

Captain Monneuse's deployment of the 1st/58th had Lieutenant Fabian's 1st Company on the left, Second-Lieutenant Yves Rigeade's 3rd Company on the right and Lieutenant Géromini's 2nd Company in reserve. The heavy weapons of Lieutenant André Tardan's 4th Company were shared out between the other three companies.

25 February 1945

At about 0500 hours on the morning of 25 February, a fresh Siberian division attacked the 2nd/57th, relieving the red Polish units hitherto engaged, and overran the French position. Captain Obitz withdrew foot by foot, while asking for support, but the inopportune withdrawal of an SS Latvian unit exposed his left flank and the situation became critical. Too thinly dispersed over the ground, the 2nd/57th was torn apart by the enemy attack, although the isolated companies fought well at the cost of heavy casualties. Cut off from the rest of his company, Officer-Cadet Million-Rousseau was last seen for an instant fighting alone in the midst of the Russians.

Captain Obitz was obliged to withdraw his battalion along the railway line, uncovering in his turn the left flank of the 1st/58th and provoking the evacuation of Bärenwalde, for which he was subsequently relieved of his command by SS-General Krukenberg.

Because of the withdrawal of the 2nd/57th on the previous evening with a view to establishing a continuous front with the 1st and 2nd Battalions of the 57th Regiment, Captain de Bourmont commanding the 57th Regiment had ordered Lieutenant Fenet to pull out of Heinrichswalde to the level of the lake midway between Barkenfelde and Bärenwalde. For lack of other means of communication, the order had been given to a mounted messenger, none other than Lieutenant de Londaize, the adjutant of the 57th Regiment.

However, the situation was evolving very fast and a new push meanwhile had obliged the 2nd/57th to withdraw to Bärenwalde, and when the 1st/57th reached its prescribed positions in the middle of the night, after having got away from Heinrichswalde without difficulty, it again found it impossible to establish contact with the 2nd/57th on their left or the Latvians on their right.

Towards 0715 hours, a patrol from the 3rd Company, 1st/58th, brought the 2nd Company, 1st/57th, an order to withdraw signed by Captain de Bourmont. The 1st/57th was to withdraw under cover of darkness to the north by a new route to some 500m parallel to Bärenwalde to receive new instructions.

At the same time, the Russian infantry moved into the attack against the 1st/57th breaching the centre of the line and threatening to split the battalion in two. To prevent this and chase the Russians off, Lieutenant Fenet collected all his available forces on the right wing of the battalion and counterattacked immediately along the line of the front.

The counterattack succeeded and while the battalion was regrouping not far from Bärenwalde, contact was established with the 1st/58th defending the edge of the woods in liaison with elements of the 15th SS-Latvian Division. At about 1100 hours Lieutenant Fenet learnt that orders had been issued at 0800 hours for him to return to Bärenwalde, where fierce fighting had been going on all morning.

At about 0600 hours, the first Russian reconnaissance units made contact with the 1st/58th and were vigorously repelled. The first proper attack took place at 0900 hours and was also checked with the loss of a few casualties. Although the battalion had contact with the 2nd/57th on the left, with which its initial forward positions were aligned, it had no contact with anyone on the right, neither German, Latvian, 1st/57th, nor even Rigeade's 3rd Company, which had been detached to occupy a position to the southeast. The 1st/58th thus had no protection on its right flank.

Captain Monneuse therefore ordered Lieutenant Tardan to make contact with the 3rd Company. Lieutenant Tardan took with him his command group and a section of mortars under Sergeant Salmon, and spent 2 hours searching for it in vain. Then, seeing elements of the 1st/57th and Latvians coming back, he sent the mortar section to opposite Bärenwalde along the Neustettin–Schlochau railway line, which was being organised as the second line of defence.

Several violent attacks developed on the 1st/58th's front during the course of the morning, but, after enduring the heavy opening bombardments, the battalion was able to check all the Russian attacks. The 1st/57th played its part late in the morning when it came under flanking fire from the heavy weapons of the Russian infantry. Once it had stopped an attack, it continued on its way.

But the enemy had more success in the 2nd/57th's sector, breaking all contact between the 1st/58th and the 2nd/57th. The Soviets occupied Bärenwalde and infiltrated the rear of the 1st/58th, obliging Captain Monneuse to withdraw in turn. Being delayed, he ordered Lieutenant Géromini's 2nd Company to open a passage and then provide a rearguard for the battalion's withdrawal.

The 2nd Company's attack proved irresistible and all the heavy weapons got through without incident except for two 75mm guns, the carriages of which had been damaged and were made unserviceable. All the wounded were carried out on the men's backs to the new position along the railway line.

It was almost noon when the vanguard of the 1st/57th came into sight of Bärenwalde and found that the village was already occupied by Russian tanks. The 1st/57th then made a half turn to resume contact with the 1st/58th, but some members of that battalion encountered on the way said that there had just been another Russian attack, more violent than before and supported by flame-throwers, which had completely disorganised the defence.

With the Russians occupying Bärenwalde and advancing along the Heinrichswalde road to Hammerstein, Fenet's 1st/57th was in danger of being encircled. To avoid this, the battalion marched westwards under cover of the woods that occupied a large part of the terrain between Bärenwalde and Hammerstein, and arrived at the camp at nightfall having sustained another two attacks on the way.

Second-Lieutenant Rigeade's 3rd Company of the 1st/58th had occupied the position designated, well away from the remainder of the battalion, at night and without prior reconnaissance, in liaison with the 15th SS-Latvian Division. The first Russian attack occurred at 0900 hours on the 25th. The Latvians dug in on the right were soon located by the enemy and, coming under heavy mortar fire, quickly withdrew. Believing that they had swept aside all resistance, the Russian infantry continued to advance but had to retire rapidly when they came under surprise fire from the well-camouflaged 3rd Company.

Then elements of the 1st/57th passed by, coming from the south as they withdrew towards Bärenwalde. Now isolated without contact to either left or right, Second-Lieutenant Rigeade was withdrawing his company on the road to Bärenwalde when two tanks with infantry escorts emerged from the woods on his right. The latter were engaged with automatic fire and one tank was damaged by a *Panzerfaust*, but the company was split into three groups, which then made their way through the woods to reach Bärenhütte.

The withdrawal of the 2nd/57th was covered by the infantry guns of the regimental company and the heavy weapons of Second-Lieutenant Philippe Colnion's 8th Company deployed alongside the railway line, as well as a combat team from Second-Lieutenant Brunet's 6th Company. The remains of the 2nd/57th, in some disarray, had to regroup behind the railway line to the left of Bärenwalde station, which served as the rough boundary with the 1st/58th, of which there was still no news, and the first elements of which had yet to withdraw.

Towards midday on 25 February, as Brigadier Puaud and SS-Colonel Zimmermann watched from the front line, the Russians launched a new attack. Despite the incredible ravage caused to this human tide, the wave of attackers advanced steadily and some twenty tanks emerged from Bärenwalde with the support of ground-assault aircraft. The 6th Company of the 2nd/57th, which had not yet completed its withdrawal, put up a magnificent defence, and was able to break contact thanks to the very heavy and precise fire from Captain Robert Roy's infantry gun company, which stopped the enemy and allowed the withdrawal to take place.

A total of four enemy tanks were destroyed. The first by an NCO using a *Panzerfaust*, the second by a mine placed by the regiment's engineer section, the two others by the regimental 75mm anti-tank guns that were old training pieces towed into position by a tractor taken from the Latvians. However, these guns were soon silenced and rendered useless. Officer-Cadet Vincenot, who was directing their fire, was seriously injured as a result of this violent enemy fire, and Lieutenant Flacy was wounded by a tank shell.

But the enemy started gaining ground and losses were heavy. The position became untenable and, after an hour of fighting, Captain de Bourmont was obliged to give the order to withdraw at the very moment that the first elements of the 1st/58th pulled back on the right wing.

The 2nd/57th was the first to set off to the north towards Elsenau, but its 7th and 8th Companies remained isolated north of the road and railway. Cut off, they retired fighting all the way to Elsenau. Lieutenant Artus, the regimental adjutant, was killed by a burst of fire. As a result of the last attack, an important breach had been made in the centre of the regiment's lines several hundred metres from the railway station, dislocating the units. The withdrawal was confused and the seriously wounded had to be abandoned. The officers, without exception, stayed behind to cover the men's withdrawal.

On a bend in the road at the bottom of a ravine, 300m along the way, elements of the 1st and 2nd Companies of the 58th had set up an anti-tank ambush, just in time to catch the first Russian tank surging through. It was destroyed with a hit from a *Panzerfaust*, probably fired by Lieutenant Fatin, while Sergeant Robert destroyed another by the same means.

Held back by this action, Lieutenants Fatin and Géromini with some of their men lost contact with the remainder of the 1st/58th and followed Captain de Bourmont, who, with the remainder of the 2nd/57th, withdrew to the divisional command post at Elsenau. This village was held by the Inspectorate's small Honour Guard and Training Company, commanded by SS-Lieutenant Wilhelm Weber.

Although the remains of the 2nd/57th retiring on Elsenau had been mostly caught, scattered and bypassed by the Russian tanks advancing on the village, 400–500 men led by several officers, including Major Boudet-Gheusi, Captain Renault, Lieutenants Weber and Fatin, managed to organise a defence. The nucleus of the defence was formed by Lieutenant Weber's company of about eighty men, which lost a quarter of its effectives but destroyed three enemy tanks. The remains of the 7th and 8th Companies of the 57th fought with equal bravery, especially in the village cemetery, where man-to-man fighting took place. The four anti-tank guns destroyed several tanks. The fighting was relentless and the Russians only made progress with difficulty. They eventually succeeded in taking the cemetery, where they killed all the injured, including a French prisoner from the 1939/40 war, who had voluntarily joined the unit. There were some on the Russian side, probably Poles, who called out rudely in excellent French for the men to surrender.

The Soviet forces engaged here in the push up to the Baltic Coast consisted of the 40th and 136th Guards Rifle Corps of the 2nd Byelorussian Front's 19th Army, temporarily supported by the 8th Guards Mechanised Corps and 3rd Guards Cavalry Corps of the 1st Byelorussian Front's 1st Guards Tank Army, Marshal Zhukov having loaned these formations to Marshal Rokossovsky on the condition that they would be returned intact!

During the course of this operation, the commander of the 19th Army was sacked for failing to keep pace with the armoured elements.

After the fall of Elsenau on the afternoon of the 25th, Russian tanks hooked round and attacked the rear of the French positions from the north, while Russian infantry blocked the escape route to the west. A group of eighty survivors, without ammunition or supplies, formed up and retreated to the north under the command of Lieutenant Fatin of the 1st/58th. With other stragglers, this constituted a company of 120 men in 3 platoons on the orders respectively of Officer-Cadets Chatrousse and Lapard, and Sergeant-Major Bonnafous. Following a painful march with the Russian tanks on their heels, they succeeded in joining up with a detachment commanded by Captain Obitz, and then Captain Martin. (The fate of this detachment will be dealt with later.)

As the Russians were advancing on Elsenau, SS-Colonel Zimmermann called on the command post of the XVIIIth Mountain Corps at Stegers to discuss the situation with General Hans Hochbaum. It was decided that the *Charlemagne* would withdraw to Stegers, while the command post of the XVIIIth Mountain Corps would withdraw to Flötenstein. At the end of the conference, General Hochbaum accompanied SS-Colonel Zimmermann to his command post's garden gate just as the first Russian tank went past and shot up and set on fire SS-Colonel Zimmermann's staff car. However, that night the corps command post managed to escape under cover of darkness and re-establish itself in Flötenstein as planned.

Next morning SS-Major-General Krukenberg met up with SS-Colonel Zimmermann at the corps command post in Flötenstein. Before departing for Neustettin, where the bulk of the Division was located, Krukenberg gave orders to SS-Colonel Zimmermann and SS-Second-Lieutenant Patzak to go to Greifenberg to arrange the departure of the replacement battalion to fill the gaps in the *Charlemagne* following these first engagements.

The 1st/58th, which was withdrawing west along the railway line to Bärenhütte, had difficulty maintaining its cohesion under fire from Russian tanks. That morning Captain Berrier's 2nd/58th arrived complete and intact at Hammerstein, where it was joined by the remainder of the 2nd/57th and 1st/58th coming from Bärenwalde. The 3rd Company of the 58th was able to organise the defence of Bärenhütte, where Captain Raybaud had established the command post of his 1st/58th. This village became a strongpoint defended by four combat teams, two provided by the 2nd/58th under Captain Berrier, one from the 1st/58th under Captain Monneuse, and the last by Captain Roy from the 58th Regiment.

During the disastrous afternoon of the 25th, while the bulk of the enemy forces were putting everything into pushing north and overwhelming Elsenau, disdaining the road from Bärenhütte to Hammerstein, a light Russian reconnaissance vehicle was stopped by the outposts in front of Bärenhütte, the vehicle and a machine gun destroyed and several prisoners taken. The German second-lieutenant serving as liaison officer to the 57th Regiment was hit by two explosive bullets in the arm and was evacuated.

The village being situated outside their main line of advance, the Russians ignored Bärenhütte, their interminable columns moving on Elsenau. By 2000 hours, the whole of the infantry guns and anti-tank guns under Captain Roy had exhausted all their ammunition on these columns, which also became the target of the mortars of the 58th Regiment's 4th and 8th Companies, provoking a Russian artillery riposte on Bärenhütte.

It was not until 2300 hours on the 25th that the Russians launched the first attack on the village, which they had encircled after nightfall. Majors de Vaugelas and Raybaud meanwhile prepared the methodical disengagement of their commands, which was to take place at midnight. The 58th Regiment's 5th Company, under Sergeant-Major Eric Walter, was given the task of engaging the enemy during the move and of forming the rearguard there-after.

As there were no means of evacuating them, the heavy guns were spiked and abandoned, and each man was given a *Panzerfaust* to carry. At the set hour the disengagement began under the direct orders of Brigadier Puaud along the only route still practicable, but which Russian patrols had tried to control several times during the evening. This was how Lieutenant Labuze, who had been sent on a liaison mission to Hammerstein, fell victim to an enemy patrol while passing through Geglenfelde.

From the beginning the disengagement took place so noisily that the Russians could not have helped noticing but, unaware of the weakness of the opposition, they failed to take advantage and kept a respectable distance, even though they could have inflicted a bloody blow by attacking the column as it withdrew.

The first elements of the Division began retreating to Neu-stettin at 1900 hours, a town about 18km west of Hammerstein.

26 February 1945

By 0300 hours the retreat was complete, except for one small combat team formed in the camp the previous evening with all available elements from the divisional headquarters and the supply column. This little company of three platoons was commanded by Major Katzian and took up a blocking position on the flanks of the axis of retreat during the night, ready to prevent the enemy infil-trating. Nothing occurred, and it withdrew at 0500 hours.

By noon, covered by the 15th SS-Latvian Division, the bulk of the *Charlemagne* had reached Neustettin, where it spent the night and took stock. Of the 4,500 men that had left Wildflecken, only 3,000 answered roll call. But the divisional headquarters and all the elements cut off at Elsenau had withdrawn to the north and northeast and, although not immediately available, could not be considered lost. This amounted to about 1,000 missing, including 15 officers, and 500 killed, including 8 officers. A total of thirty Iron Crosses were awarded for various feats of arms. The units regrouped and rested in the barracks of the town, which had not been evacuated by the civilian population.

Annoyed by the slow progress of the 19th Army, whose commander he sacked, Marshal Rokossovsky boosted the rate of advance on his left wing with the insertion of the 3rd Guards Tank Corps. Hampered by the narrow roads, the tanks nevertheless moved forward 40km that day and took the town of Baldenburg. The German XVIIIth Mountain Corps had been split apart by this thrust and the surviving elements of the *Charlemagne* had been fortunate to extricate themselves.

A report dated 0001 hours on 26 February 1945 from Staff Lieutenant-Colonel Harnack of Army Group *Weichsel*, probably gives the must lucid account of events:

The situation with the 2nd Army has deteriorated considerably. Following his attack on the XVIIIth Mountain Corps, the enemy has again pierced the corps' front and has reached Baldenburg via Stegers with his tanks. At the same time he has succeeded in dislodging and forcing back to the northwest the right wing of the XVIIIth Mountain Corps (elements of the *Charlemagne* Brigade and the 15th SS-Division).

The penetration of the thin front of the 32nd Infantry Division by the enemy cannot be reduced by the forces available to the XVIIIth Mountain Corps. We should expect the arrival of important enemy forces and an immediate change in the deployment of the Russian armies in view of the exploitation of this penetration to effect the splitting of our army group at this point.

The enemy has been able to enlarge the breach in the XVIIIth Mountain Corps' sector and push his tanks forward to Baldenburg. The 15th Waffen-Grenadier Division SS and the SS-Volunteer Brigade *Charlemagne* have thus been split into isolated combat groups, partly losing contact with their rear, and have thus practically entirely lost their combat effectiveness.

The Russians entered Hammerstein at 1700 hours on the 26th.

Chapter Three

Withdrawal

26 February 1945

The *Charlemagne*'s 15th rail transport, under the command of Captain Bassompierre, arrived at Neustettin at noon on the 26th with several other officers, bringing with them some of the guns of the artillery group from Bohemia-Moravia, and Second-Lieutenant Fayard's Flak Company from Bachrain.

Unloading was still in progress when Soviet aircraft attacked Neustettin railway station. Within 4 minutes the flak had set up its guns and set a biplane on fire, which discouraged the rest. The unloading of the artillery having been completed under the orders of Second-Lieutenant Daffas, the empty train was soon occupied by retreating German units. Then at 1800 hours, German Captain Roeming's armoured train arrived at the station.

As a result of the events of the previous day, the *Charlemagne* was now re-allocated to General von Tettau's corps on the 3rd Panzer Army's eastern wing.

27 February 1945

At about 0100 hours orders were given to embark all the artillery pieces on a train leaving for Belgard, where the Division was to regroup. The 15th SS-Latvian Division as rearguard had been forced back and an incursion by enemy tanks were feared. In fact, the alarm went off at 0300 hours and one could hear the roar of engines and tank tracks. Fortunately, under cover provided by the armoured train from behind the station, the guns were loaded on the available wagons and just as the enemy was launching his first attack at about 0700 hours, the armoured train hitched up the wagons and eventually reached Kolberg via Bublitz and Köslin.

At the same time, as planned, the first elements of the *Charlemagne* left the barracks, while the panic-stricken civilian population only began leaving just as the first Russian tanks started surrounding Neustettin from the north, cutting the railway line to Kolberg and threatening to turn the retreat into a disaster. The troops had less than an hour in which to winkle their way out. Fortunately, the enemy was none too keen from the beginning and failed to exploit the error of having two regiments concentrated into such a little area.

There was still no news of SS-Major-General Krukenberg, who had been cut off from the bulk of the Division since before Elsenau.

Towards 0800 hours the last units prepared to leave in their turn after the rest of the column, just as Colonel Kropp, the Fortress Commandant of Neustettin and charged with the defence of the town with elements of the *Pommern* Division of General von Tettau's corps, came to ask Brigadier Puaud to provide him with a battalion to assist him control the town until evening so as to hold back the enemy to enable the civilian population and those units not engaged to retire. But his constituent battalions had already left, and Brigadier Puaud only had with him some of his headquarters staff, so he gave his liaison officer, Lieutenant Auphan, the task of quickly forming an emergency march battalion from the last units in the column to hold back the enemy and allow the Division to take the field.

In fact, during the early morning, the lights and sounds of fighting coming from northeast of the town could already be distinguished, giving the impression of a more daring approach by the enemy on the bulk of the Division.

Lieutenant Auphan's improvised march battalion consisted of Second-Lieutenant Fayard's Flak Company, which had been surprised by the Russian attack as it finished loading its guns on wagons at the station, and had since been employed as infantry,

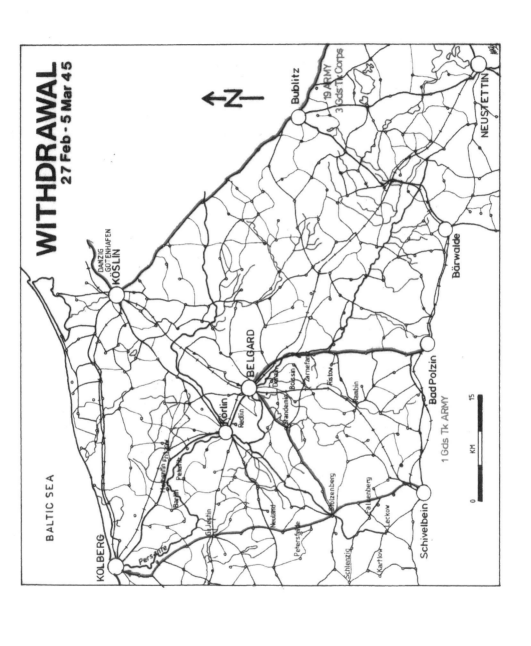

WITHDRAWAL
27 Feb - 5 Mar 45

BALTIC SEA

KOLBERG

DANZIG
GOTENHAFEN
KÖSLIN

Bublitz

19 ARMY
3 Gds Tk Corps

NEUSTETTIN

BELGARD

Körlin

Redlin

Bärwalde

Brandenberg
Dünzig
Bolssin
Zarnefanz
Ristow
Gambin

Bad Polzin

1 Gds Tk ARMY

Stölzenberg

Falkenberg
Leckow

Schivelbein

Schlenzig
Kartlow

Petersfelde

Neuland

Gr Jestin

Barin
Petershö
Hessdorf in Fritzow

Persante

0   KM   15

together with the 58th Regiment's 9th (Tank-Hunting) Company under Sergeant-Major Girard, and Lieutenant Tardan's 4th Company of the same regiment. These last two units were exhausted from the previous fighting, but there was no other solution. The battalion thus consisted of 3 officers and about 250 men.

Having assessed the situation regarding the Flak Company and established liaison to right and left with the two Wehrmacht battalions between which the French were to be inserted, and having reconnoitred the 1,200m sector assigned to him, Lieutenant Auphan decided that the position could be held by two companies, the Flak in the north and the 4th Company in the south, both companies being reinforced by two sections of tank-hunters armed with *Panzerfausts*. This deployment would enable him to keep a little reserve of about one-and-a-half sections.

Lieutenant Auphan then ordered the 4th Company, which was deployed near the barracks close to the town's western exit, to withdraw to the Flak Company's position on the flank, where it was engaged outside the artillery barracks. When Lieutenant Tardan rejoined Second-Lieutenant Fayard, the latter was having great trouble avoiding enemy fire with the last of his men. By this time the Flak Company had already lost 40 of its 130 effectives. The two companies then occupied the prescribed position in the centre of the deployment.

However, the Russian tanks, stopped about 400m from the town, were covering the anti-tank positions with their fire. It was not until about 2030 hours that aircraft bombed the town and the Russians attempted to infiltrate it. In spite of support from aircraft, artillery and mortars, the Russians were unable to make any progress. The Russian tanks were stopped by the barricades and their infantry infiltrating through the gardens came under murderous fire from riflemen posted on the roofs, in the windows and cellar exits, the whole day passing in extremely violent street fighting.

Finally abandoning the idea of a frontal attack, the enemy then attempted an encircling movement to envelop Neustettin. The French were deployed on the hill outside and enjoyed a relative calm until about 1600 hours, while to the north and south of them the German battalions were in direct contact with the enemy. A territorial battalion was holding the station area in the northern sector, but was fighting without ardour, and the officers had to intervene forcibly several times to make their men hold out. They could not give ground, even though directly menaced and having a line of retreat. In the southern sector, a Russian tank attack succeeded in reaching the barricade on the road from Tempelburg and a furious fight broke out. The Germans knocked out two tanks and the attack was repelled with heavy losses among the Russian infantry. But at 1700 hours the enemy succeeded in taking the bridge across the railway and occupying the station, while in the southern sector their cavalry came round the lake bordering the town on which the defence was anchored. The encirclement had been completed in an hour!

Colonel Kropp, the town commandant, then decided to withdraw his units, starting with the battalion defending the station sector on the left wing, with the battalion on the right wing acting as a rearguard and withdrawing by echelons to the fortified *Pommern Stellung* line at Bärwalde, 10km west of the town, where they would await the withdrawal of other German units to this new line of resistance.

Of this engagement, Lieutenant Auphan later reported:

As soon as the order was received, the battalion on the left retreated in disorder, while the battalion on the right, which was meant to act as the rearguard, did not even wait for the order and pulled out well before my battalion retired last into the town. The rally point was the command post of the German regiment, five kilometres from the town on the Bad Polzin road, where the German colonel was supposed to be expecting his units.

The German colonel had fled with his baggage,

abandoning maps, papers and telephone. Soon afterwards the command post was hit by a volley of mortar bombs and bursts of machine-gun fire coming from the direction of the lake.

I therefore decided to follow the retreat to Bärwalde, but two sections sent ahead as scouts reported that the route was already cut by Russians occupying the first village. It was hardly possible to engage them, but the railway line appeared clear, so that was the route decided upon. Pursued by the enemy, the battalion passed through a barrage of missiles, splitting into two detachments, Fayard's on a railway engine, and Auphan-Tardan's, which continued on foot.

Both rejoined the Division at Körlin.

Lieutenant Tardan's report on the same episode ran:

When the fighting stated at the barricade on the Tempelburg road, I left my command post and went forward. Half an hour later, when the fighting had died down, I went back to my command post and found only my liaison staff. The machine-gun section and the mortars that had been kept in reserve had disappeared in the direction of Bad Polzin. There was no one at all at Lieutenant Auphan's command post!

I therefore went to the command post of the German colonel in charge of the defence of the town, where I learnt that the Flak and Tank-Hunting Companies had left their positions to retreat to Bad Polzin.

Not knowing exactly what had happened, and as the encirclement had been completed and the noise of fighting coming from the southwest and the west, and that the road to Bad Polzin was cut five kilometres from Neustettin, I went back to my men.

Being the last of the Division with 60 men of the 4th Company, the commander under whose orders it had been placed having retired, and Brigadier Puaud having said on the previous day that this was only a retarding action and not an outright defence, I ordered my men to leave their positions.

Between 1800 hours on 27 February and 1100 hours on 1 March, Lieutenant Auphan's 4th Company of the 1st/58th Regiment had to march 63km to reach Bad Polzin, being obliged to make several detours to avoid the Russian vanguards. At Bad Polzin the 4th Company was fed and supplied with ammunition at the local command post and rested for 40 hours. Having been rejoined by Lieutenant Auphan, the company then left for Belgard at 0600 hours on 3 March, rejoining the Division at Körlin at 1600 hours that day.

Meanwhile, those elements of the Division that had left Neustettin directed by Captain de Perricot, the acting Chief-of-Staff, continued their retreat to Belgard via Bärwalde and Bad Polzin, a distance of 72km. On the way they discovered that the much-lauded fortified position known as the *Pommern Stellung* was, at least around Bärwalde, unmanned.

At about 1400 hours on 27 February they came under serious machine-gunning from enemy aircraft, but losses were minimal, despite the dropping of 10kg bombs, followed by a miscellany of missiles no doubt recovered from a Tsarist arsenal, that included boxes of glass grenades crammed with darts and incendiary devices. The Ruskoné section of Lieutenant Wagner's 7th of the 58th, which was marching at the tail of the column, managed to shoot down one of the aircraft with an automatic rifle.

In the middle of the night of the 27th/28th an hour's rest was taken in Bad Polzin in falling snow and a glacial wind. After marching for the rest of the night and having passed on the way several meagre armoured elements, towards 0600 hours the vanguard of the column reached an area several kilometres south of Belgard, where regrouping and reorganisation were to take place.

28 February 1945

Various elements of the *Charlemagne* kept arriving all day on the 28th, including SS-Major-General Krukenberg, who had come from Elsenau via Flötenstein and Köslin.

It had originally been intended that the reorganisation of the *Charlemagne* would take place at Köslin, an important town on the edge of the Baltic, but this town was already being threatened by Marshal Rokossovsky's tanks, which had been advancing along the axis Baldenburg–Bublitz–Köslin since the fighting at Hammerstein. Köslin was in fact taken by the Russians on the evening of 2 March, thus shutting off the immense pocket of Danzig-Gothenhafen held by the German 2nd Army. The Soviet tanks then turned off east along the Baltic coast via Stolp and Neustadt.

1 March 1945

Marshal Zhukov had launched his attack to clear the western half of Pomerania on the morning of 1 March with elements of his 1st Byelorussian Front, taking the Germans by surprise as the 1st Guards Tank Army on his right flank headed straight for Kolberg on the Baltic Coast.

2 March 1945

On 2 March, SS-Major-General Krukenberg tasked Major Emile Raybaud with forming a march regiment from the most dependable elements of the 57th and 58th Regiments, as the local situation was becoming more and more critical. This difficult task was achieved in 10 hours. The remainder were then formed into a Reserve Regiment under Captain de Bourmont, but the fighting value of this latter regiment was greatly reduced through the troops' extreme state of fatigue.

At about 1000 hours, Brigadier Puaud, accompanied by his staff (Major de Vaugelas, Captain Renault and Lieutenant Delille) made a motor reconnaissance of the banks of the Persante, a little river flowing through the towns of Belgard and Körlin and on to the Baltic at Kolberg. The aim of the reconnaissance was to find the crossing points before deploying blocking units. That same evening the divisional headquarters were established in Schloss Kerstin, northeast of Körlin.

At about 1800 hours the Divisional Headquarters received the order to move immediately to the little town of Körlin to stop and hold the Russian advance, and specifically to protect the withdrawal to the port of Kolberg of the troops in Pomerania.

The move was undertaken at night in a certain amount of confusion, leading to abnormal delays in the deployment of the companies after their arrival at Körlin. The unexpected arrival from Greifenberg of the Division's 500-strong Field Replacement Battalion led by Captain Michel Bisiau next day enabled the provision of a third company for each provisional battalion and brought their establishments up to 750 men each.

3 March 1945

At dawn on 3 March the *Charlemagne*, now more than 4,000 strong, took up positions in the little town of Körlin and the surrounding villages in the worst of atmospheric conditions, an icy blizzard. The Division now came under Major-General Oskar Munzel's corps, covering the sector Köslin–Belgard–Kolberg, with headquarters at Belgard.

During the move of the column through Belgard, General Krukenberg had briefed Major Raybaud that the *Charlemagne* was to adopt a defensive position along the Persante River facing east, presenting a barrier to the enemy on the main road from Köslin to Stettin. In fact Körlin formed a strong natural defensive position, being surrounded on three sides by the Persante and a tributary that restricted access to the town to a few bridges that could easily be defended.

At 0800 hours the order was given for the evacuation of the civilian population. Major Raybaud was appointed battle commandant of the town of Körlin, and set up his command post in a house on the main square. The March Regiment would have its centre of gravity here, while the Reserve Regiment covered the crossing points of the Persante north of the town with the 1st Battalion at Barlin, Mechentin and Peterfilz, and the 2nd Battalion deployed further out.

Hard fighting broke out at about 1500 hours. Some of this was in the Köslin sector, necessitating intervention by *Stuka* dive-bombers and tanks, some of the latter being captured on the Körlin–Köslin road. Danger was thus threatening from the northeast. Meanwhile, in the southeast, a powerful Russian column, subjected to counterattacks on its flank by German tanks, advanced more slowly from Bad Polzin to Belgard, coming up against a strong defence from the Wehrmacht, and drawing attention in this direction.

To counter the first danger, the 2nd Battalion of the March Regiment under Captain Bassompierre covered the town from the northeast, either side of the Köslin road, while Lieutenant Fenet's 1st Battalion prepared to meet the other threat from the southeast astride the road leading from Körlin to Belgard.

Then at about 1800 hours Divisional Headquarters was advised of a strong mechanised Russian concentration reported in the Stolzenberg area, thus posing a third potential, if not immediate, threat. Then at about 2000 hours came the news that a strong armoured Soviet column of ninety tanks and about two motorised regiments of infantry (the 45 Guards Tank Brigade of the 11th Guards Tank Corps, 1st Guards Tank Army) was moving out of Stolzenberg towards Kolberg. The fall of this port would threaten the encirclement and annihilation of the *Charlemagne*, as well as the *Munzel* Corps and all the other diverse elements still to be found in the Kolberg–Köslin–Belgard area. Also moving out of Stolzenburg, the 1st Guards Tank Brigade was heading for Belgard and Körlin.

Divisional Headquarters moved to Körlin on the night of the 3rd/4th. The sounds of battle could be heard, and the lights seen, to the southeast, but also to the southwest, which was disquieting, as the defensive system had been organised along the right bank of the Persante.

4 March 1945

The vanguard of tanks of the column coming from Stolzenberg took the village of Gross Jestin, 5km south of Kolberg and 15km northeast of Belgard at 0200 hours on the 4th, moving at such a speed that several elements of the *Charlemagne*, the motorised supply column and the pioneer section of the Greifenberg Battalion were almost caught there. They had not been alerted by their sentries, and only just managed to escape to the northwest towards Treptow-an-der-Rega. By 0500 hours, the leading tanks of this same column were in front of Kolberg, which they invested, forming a pocket incarcerating the *Munzel* Corps and a good part of the *von Tettau* Group.

During the course of the morning, some of these Soviet elements fell back towards the east and fell upon Körlin, attempting to reduce the Belgard–Körlin pocket in cooperation with the forces attacking Köslin from the northeast and those approaching Belgard from Bad Polzin in the southeast. The Pomeranian front had collapsed and the 3rd Panzer Army penetrated at several points. Further south, the remains of the Xth SS-Corps were encircled in another pocket.

The *Charlemagne*'s Divisional Headquarters withdrew from Körlin, now directly threatened from three sides at once, and with the Division's units already in contact with the enemy, to establish itself at Schloss Fritzow, several kilometres north of Körlin on the Kolberg road, where the command post of Captain de Bourmont's Reserve Regiment was already located. The latter then moved to the Klaptow Domain.

Towards midday, with still no sign of enemy tanks on the outskirts of Körlin, none having been signalled, and with no alarm from the outposts to the west, Major Raybaud set off for the Persante Bridge on the outskirts of the town to remind the German engineers tasked with demolishing it not to take action without formal orders from him. This bridge was necessary to enable the withdrawal of the outposts, about a company's worth, and also to enable expected reinforcements of German tanks coming from the west to enter the town.

Examining the terrain from horseback, Major Raybaud saw a tank hull-down about a kilometre away behind a hump in the road, but was unable to determine its nationality. At the same moment, the first shell exploded, severely wounding Major Raybaud in the right knee and fracturing his left tibia in two places. The *Charlemagne* was unfortunately lacking in medical facilities. Captain Durandy, the Divisional Medical Officer, decided to evacuate the two worst wounded, including Major Raybaud, to Kolberg in a liaison vehicle. Although the Russians had already intercepted traffic on that route several times that morning, by some lucky chance the liaison vehicle got through safely. The two wounded men were eventually evacuated by sea after being treated at a casualty collecting post in Kolberg, which was already under Russian attack.

At about 1230 hours the first Russian elements, estimated at about twenty-five tanks supported by two companies of infantry, deployed from the southwest along the west bank of the Persante and attacked Körlin at its southeast exit. The bridge was blown and three enemy tanks were destroyed in a few minutes by a *Tiger* tank which appeared there at an opportune moment. This brought the Soviet attack to a temporary halt.

Captain de Perricot, who had taken over the temporary command of the regiment while awaiting the arrival of Captain Bassompierre to succeed Major Raybaud, was also slightly wounded. The Russian tanks brought the whole of the southern part of Körlin under fire, stopping traffic on the road and bridge to Belgard, where refugees were fleeing back under fire from the machine guns of Soviet aircraft.

Meanwhile the *Charlemagne*'s Divisional Headquarters had received orders from the *Reichsführer-SS* at Army Group *Weichsel* to hold Körlin at all costs, as the town was to form the pivot of withdrawal for all the German troops in the region. Lieutenant Defever's 2nd Reserve Battalion came forward to reinforce the west front of Körlin, where the danger was the most pressing. The Greifenberg companies withdrew by their battalions and were engaged in the defence on the west side of the town. At about 1430 hours, enemy infantry crossed the Persante at several places and established footholds on the right bank, directly threatening the rear of Lieutenant Fenet's 1st March Battalion and taking the southeastern defence of Körlin in the rear.

So, at about 1500 hours, Lieutenant Fenet's battalion turned about, emerged from the village of Redlin, and counterattacked towards the western edges of Körlin, taking the enemy in the flank. This threw back the infiltrated Soviet infantry, despite their supporting fire, and thus allowed the withdrawal of the advance units behind the Persante that had been previously unable to move. Once the counterattack was over, Fenet's battalion returned to its original positions in Redlin.

Towards 1600 hours, part of the supply column was sent off to Kolberg, a reconnaissance patrol from the artillery battalion having reported the road again free. The patrol had got as far as the city gates at about 1400 hours, and found the Russians few in number but well equipped and already occupying the mill and the bridge over the first arm of the Persante. Before the patrol returned via Fritzow, Sergeant-Major Ranc and Gunners Blaise and Hoinard destroyed a lone Russian tank with a *Panzerfaust*.

A meeting was held at Divisional Headquarters at 1800 hours at which were present General Krukenberg, Brigadier Puaud, Major Vaugelas, Captains Schlisler and de Perricot, and Lieutenants Huan and Tardan. It was decided to hold on at whatever the cost. But the news coming in was far from encouraging. In fact, Headquarters 3rd Panzer Army at Plathe, which had yet to be threatened by the enemy, had intended securing the *von Tettau* Group and reinforcing the *Munzel* Corps, while hardening the front from Stettin to Belgard with elements of the 10th SS-Panzer Division *Frundsberg*, but were unable to do so for lack of fuel.

Only a vanguard formed from the armoured reconnaissance group of the IIIrd SS-Panzer Corps, consisting of six light armoured vehicles, a radio vehicle, two vehicles with guns and another two with machine guns, managed to reach the Neuland crossroads, where the Köslin–Körlin–Plathe and Schivelbein–Stolzenberg–Kolberg roads met some 15km southeast of Körlin. Here it encountered an outpost of the *Charlemagne*, Second-Lieutenant Pignard-Berthet and eighty men of the 1st March Company from Greifenberg, whose link with the rear had just been cut off by the Russian advance. This little mixed unit tried to reach Körlin, but was soon repelled by the Russians and dispersed, only to be annihilated after destroying three tanks and killing ten men in an ambush.

Following a new radio contact with the *Reichsführer-SS* at Army Group *Weichsel*, General Krukenberg and Brigadier Puad decided to break through to the west in several echelons. The 3rd Panzer Army's main withdrawal zone was approximately on the line Greifenberg–Plathe. However, one could neither leave Körlin by the northeast, the road appearing to be definitely cut, nor to the west, where Russian forces were in position. Belgard was still held by the Wehrmacht, so they would have to leave Körlin, heading southeast as far as Belgard, and then go obliquely westwards. As most of the roads in this region were already being crossed by enemy columns, the *Charlemagne* would have to follow side roads or go cross-country.

The proper execution of such an operation depended upon the cover of night, and it was decided to start evacuating Körlin at 2300 hours. Nevertheless, the *Charlemagne*'s resistance on 4 March had enabled some elements of the 3rd Panzer Army to withdraw. A delayed order to regroup near Plathe eventually reached the Division, but it was doubtful whether it was possible to do so. The order of march was determined as follows:

– Vanguard: Divisional HQ with Lieutenant Fenet's 1st March Battalion.

– Main Body: Captain de Bourmont's Reserve Regiment
with the *Monneuse* and *Defever* Battalions.
– Rearguard: Captain Bassompierre's 2nd March Battalion.

At the conclusion of the meeting, SS-General Krukenberg,
SS-Colonel Zimmermann, and SS-Captain Jauss joined
Lieutenant Fenet's battalion, which left its positions in Redlin at
the designated time. Brigadier Puaud declined to join the
vanguard, wanting to remain until the departure of the rearguard.

Then, at about 0100 hours next day, Brigadier Puaud changed
his mind and decided to leave Körlin with Major de Vaugelas and
Captain Renault to rejoin the vanguard, wrongly believing that
this would be the most dangerous position. However, their vehicle
broke down on the Belgard road and they were then obliged to
march along with Captain de Bourmont's main body.

The vanguard column arrived at Belgard at about 0200 hours,
crossed the cemetery and circuited the burning town, the roads of
which were choked with abandoned vehicles and where a furious
battle was in progress between the Soviets and some Wehrmacht
units. The Fenet Battalion then disappeared into the countryside.

The 3,000 or so men comprising the main body of the
Charlemagne were now under the direct command of Brigadier
Puaud, assisted by Major de Vaugelas, Captains de Perricot, de
Bourmont, Schlisler, Renault and other officers. The head of this
column arrived at Belgard in its turn, but because of the extent of
the fighting going on in the town, made a half-turn and crossed the
Persante downstream from the town.

At daybreak the column found itself in a wooded area south of
Belgard where it had regrouped several days previously, and came
under artillery fire. The troops dispersed and used the cover of
dense fog to mask them from the enemy.

According to an eyewitness, Medical Lieutenant Dr Métais,
with first light a thick wood, marsh, a stream and then a wide plain
could be discerned. The edge of the woods was on either side
100m away. Brigadier Puaud was there on foot with his staff:

'What's happening. Its mad! Who's leading?'

'De Bourmont'.

Then turning towards Major de Vaugelas, the chief-of-staff, Brigadier Puaud said: 'Take a horse. Tell him to find a wood free of the enemy straight away, to stay there and to organise the defence!'

As Major de Vaugelas left for the head of the column at the gallop, Brigadier Puaud shouted: 'It's mad! I already advised him to hide in woods during daylight. If this goes on, there will be a massacre!'

Soon afterwards, at about 0800 hours, the thick fog lifted within a few minutes just as the column headed for the surrounding woods. Immediately spotted by the Russians, it was taken under a violent fire from tanks that had taken up the chase with the support of heavy weapons. The panic and massacre foreseen by Brigadier Puaud then followed. The survivors tended to make their way to the nearby woods. Several succeeded, but the majority were shot down or captured.

The rearguard formed by the Reserve Regiment, some eighty to ninety men under Lieutenant Bartolomei, arrived at Belgard at about 0700 hours. Fighting was still in progress, and Lieutenant Bartolomei considered reinforcing or relieving those elements of the *Charlemagne* that he thought were trapped there. He then came under heavy mortar fire and became disorientated, heading back to Körlin, which he had left several hours earlier and where Captain Bassompierre's 2nd March Battalion was now encircled. There too his company came under violent fire, for the Russians had completely invested Körlin. The detachment then withdrew along the Persante and crossed it by a footbridge. They were returning to Körlin along the left bank when, at about noon, they came across 3 officers and 150 men that had been scattered in that morning's disaster. Together they then decided to head for the Stettin area by night marches, but all were to be captured several days later.

At about 1400 hours, several hours after the disaster in the

Belgard woods, Brigadier Puaud was seen by some soldiers wounded on a horse. He told them to try and get through to the west. Brigadier Puaud was never seen again. It would seem that, wounded by a shot in the leg, he had succeeded with the help of a group of comrades in reaching Greifenberg, where he was left in an inn with other wounded that could not be moved. He disappeared there, probably eliminated by enemy soldiers.

At about 0500 hours on the 5th, another group of about 600 men led by Second-Lieutenant Leune and Medical Lieutenants Métais and Herpe, formed up and marched westwards by night for two days, managing to rejoin the Fenet Battalion at Schloss Meseritz on the morning of 7 March.

Another detachment under Lieutenant Fayard joined up with a company of *Volkssturm* and was captured by Russian tanks on the 7th. Several other small groups tried to regain the German lines in vain.

On the morning of the 5th, a group of about 150 isolated Frenchmen and Germans collected around three self-propelled guns at Fritzow and tried to get through to Kolberg. Caught halfway in a little village by Russian tanks, they succeeded in getting away and penetrating the enemy investment of the outskirts of Kolberg. There they were directed to the Casino, where they met up with Captain Havette and about 100 sick and wounded men from the *Charlemagne*.

The situation in Kolberg was dire. Colonel Fritz Fullriede, a former farmer in South-West Africa, had arrived on 1 March to take over command of the town, which Hitler had declared a fortress to be defended to the last man. Fullriede found a garrison of 3,300 combatants, including a fortress-engineer machine-gun battalion, a training battalion and a Volkssturm battalion, a flak battalion and a train carrying six immobile tanks awaiting repair. But the peacetime population of the town had expanded from 35,000 inhabitants to 85,000. Outside the town were parked twenty-two trains that had brought refugees from all over the province, some hoping to be conveyed on to Stettin and some hoping to be taken on by ship. However, the railway authorities in Stettin had blocked further traffic into the city as it was already crammed with refugees.

When Colonel Fullriede requested the local Nazi leader to organise the evacuation of civilians from the town, he was told that the provincial Gauleiter had not given his permission, nor would he, as the orders were for the town to be held. However, Colonel Fullriede could not see how he could defend a town clogged with refugees, and decided to go ahead with their evacuation regardless and instructed SS-Brigadier Bertlin of the local Party administration to organise it.

On 5 March the first Soviet artillery shells hit the town. A combat team ordered to clear the railway line out of the town to the west next day was stalled by Soviet tanks. However, the coastal road was still open and thousands of refugees set off on foot. It is estimated that some 15,000 refugees eventually managed to get through to Swinemünde this way. For the more fortunate ones, the Luftwaffe instituted a shuttle service with flying-boats operating between the Kamper See lake near the seaside resort of Deep and their base at Parow, 7km west of Stralsund, taking thirty to thirty-five passengers at a time.

In all some 600 members of the *Charlemagne* reached Kolberg before the town was finally cut off on 7 March, the day the OKH forbade any attempt to breakout to the west by Colonel Fullriede. Many of these were from the Divisional headquarters staff and support units, but there were also some members of the Honour Company and the March Regiment, and, importantly for the defence, the 105mm howitzer battery of Regiment 57, whose commander, Captain Havette, was the senior *Charlemagne* officer in the town.

The howitzers came as a valuable contribution to the defence, whose heavy armament consisted so far of only seven heavy and eight light anti-aircraft guns and those guns on the six tanks waiting repair, which had to be manhandled into position. However, that same day naval destroyers *Z-34* and *Z-43* arrived outside the port to assist with the firepower of their 150mm guns.

The Frenchmen were accommodated in the municipal casino. At first, those that were able were employed in preparing anti-tank defences, but then Colonel Fullriede requested the provision of a combat team. Some 200–300 men were mustered for this purpose and formed into three platoons under the command of SS-Lieutenant Ludwig. This combat team, or *compagnie de marche*, was then allocated to the support of Battalion *Hempel*, being deployed on the battalion's left flank and was soon engaged in heavy street fighting. However, a considerable proportion of the remainder had been utterly demoralised by their experiences. These were disarmed and used for constructing defences and later assisting with the evacuation of the refugees.

Next day the 1st Polish Army took over the siege of the town with its 3rd and 6th Infantry Divisions from the 1st Guards Tank Army's 45th Guards Tank Brigade and 272nd Rifle Division, and additional rocket-launchers and heavy mortars were brought up to swell the bombardment of the town by some 600 guns. The Poles were later further reinforced by their 4th Infantry Division and the 4th Polish Heavy Tank Regiment.

The evacuation by sea began on the night of 11/12 March, after some large freighters had arrived in the roadstead outside the port, with smaller boats and ferries conveying the wounded and refugees out to them. Artillery support was provided by the destroyers *Z-34* and *Z-43*, now reinforced by heavy torpedo boat *T-33*. The naval vessels also joined in the evacuation, taking on refugees for transit to Swinemünde in overnight shuttles that enabled them to restock with ammunition before returning.

The Poles launched a major attack on the 13th, capturing the town gasworks upon which the fighting had been focused, and closing up to the harbour on both banks of the Persante River. Calls over the open radio by the Polish commander for the surrender of the town at 1530 and 1600 hours on the 14th were simply ignored.

On the 15th the defence received last-minute reinforcements in the form of two companies of Fortress-Regiment 5 brought in by sea against the wishes of Colonel Fullriede, who saw no need for them. These were immediately thrown into a counterattack in the area of the railway station, only to suffer heavy casualties.

The last of the civilian refugees were embarked on the night of 15/16 March. The following day the defence was reduced to an area 1,800m long by 400m deep on the east bank of the Persante, and Colonel Fullriede decided it was time to withdraw.

During the early hours of the 18 March the last troops withdrew to the ships under cover of a massive bombardment from both sides that prevented the Soviets from advancing any further. Colonel Fullriede was the last to leave of the 68,000 civilians, 1,223 wounded and 5,213 combatants evacuated by sea from Kolberg.

On 26 March Hitler personally decorated Colonel Fullriede with the Knight's Cross of the Iron Cross for this outstanding achievement.

A matron from a hospital in Kolberg gave an account of her evacuation. The roads out of the town were blocked with traffic and Soviet tanks, so she and a nursing sister made their way along the coastline to the west. Some of the other sisters from her hospital had gone ahead with the walking wounded from a Luftwaffe hospital.

> We had not eaten for a long time, so we sat down in the sand to take a short breakfast break. We were well behind the others. I quietly hoped to stay the night at the seaplane base at Deep. I also wanted to meet up again with the other sisters there. After we had clambered with great difficulty on all fours across the dunes, we were able to continue on our way. The baggage was like an iron anchor. It was 2 kilometres to the air base. Eventually we reached it. Before we got to the barracks, we heard that another aircraft was leaving that evening. We made our way to the boarding point, where we had to stand until evening with many others. Two machines took off, taking mothers with small children. Then it was said

that perhaps there would be another in the morning. After a night in the barracks, we were back at the boarding point again by 7 o'clock with hundreds of other people. The Kolberg-Dievenow passed immediately alongside the Kamper See and the flood of refugees with it. Those who could discard their baggage sought to fly. More and more aircraft arrived that took mothers with children, which was quite right. Many had been standing there since yesterday and had no milk, not even water for their children. Columns of smoke stood on the horizon, probably burning villages. Over 20 machines arrived and over 20 times we had to remain behind. That evening we were able to board a machine that took us to Swinemünde.

Chapter Four

Retreat

After the division left for Körlin on 4 March, the 2nd Battalion of the March Regiment, 600 strong and still completely surrounded in the town, continued to hold out against enemy forces considerably superior in numbers and equipment. Violently bombarded by the Russian tanks and mortars, and at about 1900 hours harassed by partisans (probably Polish workers) who threatened the command post for a moment before they were chased off and destroyed, Captain Bassompierre hoped to leave the town under cover of the coming night.

The Russians occupied the cemetery on 7 March, but were immediately chased out again by a counterattack with fixed bayonets led by Sergeant-Major Walter.

At about 1800 hours, having held out for two days with his weak battalion, Captain Bassompierre decided to try to carry out the order to rejoin the Division with the nine officers and 500 men remaining.

The order having been given, the seriously wounded were stripped of their military clothing and documents, and left in the care of the civilian German representative of the German Red Cross in Körlin. The less seriously wounded were mounted on horses, whose hooves had been wrapped in sacks to silence them, to try to move along with the column.

At about 1900 hours the vanguard under Second-Lieutenant Rigeade left the town to the east by the railway bridge under cover of a diversion on the other side of town, a barrage by all the heavy weapons to use up the last of their ammunition. Under cover of night, the battalion followed the Belgard railway line for about

4km and then slipped between the Russian lines into the woods. In fact, as a result of false information, Bassompierre believed Kolberg to have fallen, so had decided to go round Belgard by the east and south, aiming for Stettin. He marched in the middle of the column, the last troops leaving Körlin at 2200 hours. It was high time; armoured vehicles were arriving from Köslin.

There then followed a long series of marches, detours (often through woods), constant encounters with the enemy, about fifteen of them, individual acts of bravery, such as Warrant-Officer Robert saving the column trapped by Russian tanks by destroying two of them with *Panzerfausts*.

One night the battalion was obliged to cross a main road on which there was heavy enemy traffic in both directions. While crossing the road diagonally, the vanguard ran into a Russian guard-post. Then, risking all or nothing, instead of crossing by bounds, the battalion prepared to cross together by surprise. At the same moment a column of Russian assault tanks appeared. To avoid all being destroyed, the men suddenly opened up a violent fire. Within several minutes four tanks and a dozen trucks and other vehicles had been destroyed with *Panzerfausts*. Unaware of the relative weakness of their opponents, the surprised enemy fled in all directions. But the enemy reaction also cost dear; Captain Monneuse was killed and Lieutenant Dr Joubert disappeared.

Tired and hungry, the column had to abandon its wounded. One of them, a youngster of 18 and unmoveable, was finished off by his section leader. Anyone who leant against a tree fell asleep from fatigue, and anyone who fell asleep was lost.

During another fight with tanks coming out of a wood, the column was dispersed in the area north of Schievelbein. Captain Bassompierre and several survivors were captured by the Russians on 17 March.

After this dispersal, however, certain elements, guided mainly by the best NCOs of the old LVF, were able to reach the banks of the Oder, where they were captured by the enemy for lack of means to cross the river. This was the case with twenty men led by

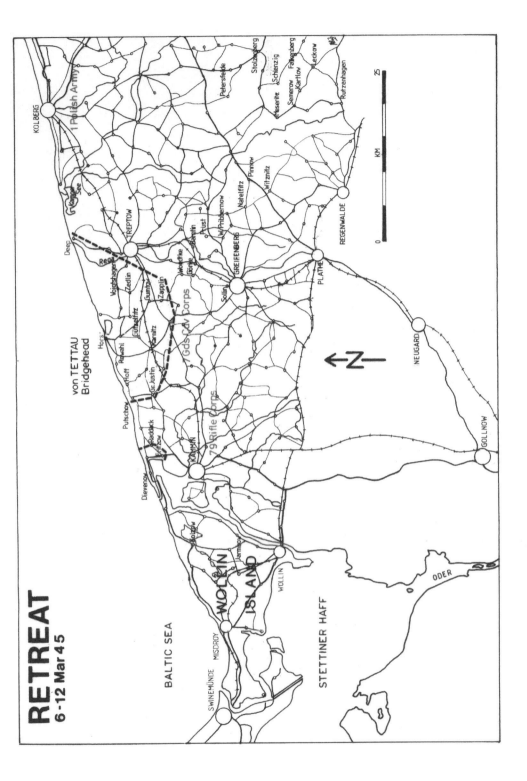

RETREAT
6-12 Mar 45

Company-Sergeant-Major Girard. Then on the night of 23/24 March, Battalion-Sergeant-Major Gobion, also ex-LVF, reached the Oder with ten men at the cost of much suffering. They tried to cross the river by the half-destroyed bridge at Wollin, found it and were fired upon, suffering three wounded, two of whom had to be abandoned. On the other bank the attention of German soldiers had been attracted by the firing. They signalled to the nine survivors and showed them where some pneumatic boats were hidden in a branch of the river, but they would have to swim to get them. One man tried but took cramp in the icy water and gave up. At dawn on the 24th, following an artillery duel from one side to the other, the Russians attacked and a group of Polish soldiers captured the nine of them in a potato store.

The vehicular column and the Divisional services that had been quartered at Gross Jestin, south of Kolberg, left at 0200 hours on 4 March with the Russian tanks on their heels, but had been able to reassemble later that morning at Treptow an der Rega. There a lone Russian soldier, who had been able to run behind the vehicles during the night and climb aboard and cause some damage, was knocked down by one of the drivers with his rifle. The column left Treptow at 0600 hours and reached the mouth of the Oder and tried to cross the river, but was unsuccessful. There were Russians swarming everywhere, and the column had another narrow escape at about 1000 hours.

Eventually the column reached the port of Swinemünde at 1100 hours on the 6th. There were about 200 men with Majors Katzian and Boudet-Gheusi, Captain Jotard, and SS-Lieutenants Meier and Weber.

Having bypassed Belgard during the night of 4/5 March, Lieutenant Fenet's 1st Battalion headed south, southwest towards Denzin after avoiding the Standemin area, which was reported strongly occupied by the Russians. The column passed within sight of Boissin, then continued in a south, southwesterly direction.

At daybreak on the 5th, the divisional commander had the soldiers spread out in a wooded area, but the harassed men had no chance to rest, for it was very cold and the snow continued to fall. Certainly there was no question of lighting a fire and forced immobility only emphasised the cold.

According to the locals, the roads and paths through the forests were permanently patrolled by cavalry during the day, so General Krukenberg had a council of war with SS-Colonel Zimmermann, SS-Captain Jauss and Lieutenant Fenet. The latter insisted that they did not wait for nightfall to continue, for the men would freeze if they did not move all day and would not be able to go on, and besides, there was no time to lose. A vast forest extended westwards and they should make use of it to march by compass during the day, avoiding the roads. General Krukenberg agreed with him.

At about 0900 hours the battalion set off again after disposing of some of its equipment too unwieldy for a march through the forest. The first difficulty occurred in crossing the Rambin–Belgard road, which was heavily guarded by Russian posts, and this was only managed by making a long detour that enabled the battalion to cross under cover of the woods at a point out of sight of the guard-posts. All this was accomplished in silence and without incident. During the morning halt, the battalion had been helped by the distant fighting developing in the Zarnefanz–Ristow–Boissin area, unaware that it involved the rest of the Division.

At nightfall the battalion left the forest and continued its march without incident. Passing to the south of Stolzenberg during the night, the column crossed the Schievelbein–Kolberg highway between Russian trucks and tanks. The column even went through a village occupied by a Russian regimental headquarters without being seen. Then men of SS-Captain Jauss's rearguard, wanting to enter a house for a drink, set off the alarm, waking the Russians, but fortunately there were no serious losses. Then the battalion passed Falkenberg, which bore traces of the fighting on the previous day between the Soviets and an armoured division of the Corps.

After 3 hours' rest at Schlenzig on 6 March, the battalion set off again, but this time the situation became worrying. Having crossed the dangerous Standemin–Stolzenberg area, it was hoped to reach Greifenberg without difficulty, but that morning civilians reported that the Russians were at Plathe, 15km southeast of Greifenberg, and that Greifenberg had been surrounded by the enemy. But it was also learnt that several kilometres away there was an estate occupied by a retired Army major and that German troops had been seen there in the past few days. However, this information could not be confirmed.

Nevertheless, the battalion made a hook to the north as far as Petersfelde, where the white flag was already flying, but there it was learnt that a Wehrmacht corps was regrouping at Meseritz, about 10km away. The battalion arrived at Meseritz as night was falling. Men and vehicles were still milling around and camping in the castle park, where the headquarters of General Munzel's Corps was located. General Munzel gave General Krukenberg his own Iron Cross First Class to award to Lieutenant Fenet.

Further east, the remains of Lieutenant-General Hans von Tettau's Corps, some 10,000–15,700 strong and consisting of 5 or more scratch divisions, including the Panzer Division *Holstein* and Division *Pommern*, had lost all radio contact with the parent 3rd Panzer Army. It broke out of encirclement in the area south of Belgard early on 5 March and started making its way towards the tiny harbour of Horst, from where von Tettau hoped to be evacuated by sea.

The men of the *Charlemagne* were able to sleep for several hours at Meseritz on the 6th, but the columns set off again through woods towards midnight to arrive at Pinnow on the Plathe–Körlin highway early in the morning.

On 7 March the column reached Natelfitz, some 10km from

Greifenberg, where it was hoped that they could relieve the surrounded German garrison. The French battalion, which was completely exhausted and had practically eaten nothing for three days, did not take part in the attack from Natelfitz. It had come to within 7km of Greifenberg before being stopped by the Russians. It was now necessary, without loss of time, to pass north of the town to reach the new rallying point at Kammin on the Oder estuary. At this point thirty men that had been lost for three days rejoined the main body.

After passing the night at Wendisch Pribbernow, the march continued on 8 March towards the northwest, but it was then reported that Kammin had been taken by the enemy. They then tried to reach the Baltic coast at the nearest point, passing the Rega near Treptow. The same day, seven men were wounded by a mine exploded by a vehicle on the Treptow–Greifenberg road. During the afternoon some fighting developed towards Görke and Woedtke, the last village having been retaken from the Soviets, who had pillaged the place and committed numerous acts of violence. During the day the battalion complimented General Krukenberg on his fifty-seventh birthday. The last night before reaching the Baltic was spent at Zapplin.

The column continued on its way without incident all day on 9 March and arrived late at the little fishing port of Horst, where it rested. The forces of Generals Munzel and von Tettau, about 50,000 strong, half of which were civilians, combined to form a bridgehead there, but hopes of evacuation by sea proved unattainable, as all available shipping resources were already employed in the evacuation of Kolberg and other ports further east.

A report submitted by a Major Kropp to Army Group *Weichsel* on 9 March 1945 stated:

Von Tettau is at Horst in a bridgehead about 20 kilometres wide and 10 kilometres deep, delimited as follows: Putshow tile factory (inclusive) - Dresow (inclusive) - Karnitz,

Klein Zapplin (inclusive) - Gumtow (inclusive) - Zedlin - Voigtshagen as far as Deep.

There are elements of the Division *Holstein* without vehicles from Horst to Gumtow inclusive; the Division *Pommern* as far as Voigtshagen inclusive; the 15th SS-Latvian Division as far as Deep.

There are about 50,000 people in the pocket, half of them civilians.

Two battalions and one battery of the 5th Light Division have arrived via Gulzow and are now near Stettin.

Armament available: 30 artillery pieces, several self-propelled 88mm anti-aircraft guns: no precise figure. No anti-tank guns, no tanks. The *Holstein* is entirely on foot.

Light enemy pressure in the von Tettau sector.

Von Tettau has established a bridgehead at Horst for evacuation by sea. Tonight he will regroup his forces to rejoin the lines in the area Dresow-Gross Justin. He will move along the coast, escorting the civilians without their baggage on the way.

Near Dievenow the road is quite bad and can easily be fired upon by the enemy.

There are no anti-tank defences in the area, neither static nor mobile.

There is only a five-ton bridge at Dievenow. A ferry will have to be established.

We have asked the navy's support to ensure the evacuation of the women and children from Horst and Rewahl.

Something has to be done to ensure that the evacuation can be carried out effectively.

With the Russians closing in, the *Charlemagne* battalion left Horst during the afternoon to reach the seaside resort of Rewahl at about 1700 hours.

Accepting the impossibility of evacuation by sea, Lieutenant-General von Tettau opted for running the Soviet gauntlet westwards along the coast to Dievenow, where German troops from the Swinemünde area were in occupation. Von Tettau being a personal friend of SS-Colonel Zimmermann, the latter succeeded in persuading him to allow the *Charlemagne* to lead the breakout of the refugees, now numbering several thousand.

At Rewahl, 10 March was meant to be a rest day, but Russian reinforcements in the form of the 7th Guards Cavalry Corps started attacking the German concentration during the day.

The breakout along the narrow beach was led by an advance party formed from members of the Fusilier Battalion of the *Holstein* Panzer Division and officer-cadet Regiment *Buchenau*. This was followed at midnight by the main body of refugees led by twenty members of the *Charlemagne* under the command of Lieutenant Fenet, who was accompanied by SS-Colonel Zimmermann to deal with any mines encountered in his capacity as an engineer. A covering party, including SS-Major-General Krukenberg, went along the top of the dunes, to try and prevent alerting enemy patrols and sentries, while the remainder of the battalion formed a rearguard with some members of the 4th SS-Police-Panzergrenadier Division. Another group commanded by Captain Roy escorted the convoy of those vehicles still remaining along the coastal road, leaving some 2 hours later.

However, the many hold-ups that occurred slowed down progress so much that after the penetration made by the advance party the Soviets had time to return and attack the main column with grenades and machine guns. (The Soviet troops involved were from the 79th Rifle Corps, which was later to gain fame in the storming of the Reichstag in Berlin.) The advance was hampered by the narrowness of the beach, which was only 1–10m wide between the sea on the right and the several metres high dunes covered in vegetation on the left.

Local counterattacks were made by the *Fenet* Battalion as it passed through. SS-Colonel Zimmermann was lightly wounded in the foot during the first encounter and continued the march wearing slippers. There were several deaths and a certain number of injured. Among those that disappeared was the medical officer, Senior Officer-Cadet Anneshaensel, who was last seen attending to the wounded.

Tasked with providing naval support, the heavy cruiser *Admiral Scheer* and the heavy torpedo-boat *T-33* started firing on the groups moving along the seashore, mistaking them for Russians, but the firing fortunately stopped when signal flares set off by the troops alerted the ships to their error.

One of the Frenchmen recalled encountering the scene of a previous Soviet attack:

> We came to a small cliff where an atrocious spectacle awaited us. Hundreds of corpses of women and children on the beach; a refugee column, surprised by the Soviets. We were struck still looking at these mutilated and naked corpses. Those young girls, mothers and grandmothers had been gang-raped one or two days previously by the victors. Then their throats had been cut and their bellies slit open.

After several encounters with the enemy, the battalion succeeded in getting through thanks to its counterattacks, and met up with the German forces guarding the approaches to Dievenow, which they eventually reached at about 0800 hours. The men were then able to rest for a few hours. They were soaked to their hips, for they often had had to wade in the sea. The battalion had evaded encirclement but was the only *Charlemagne* unit to be able to rejoin the German lines.

At about 0500 hours the coastal road convoy had had a severe engagement with alerted motorised Russian elements. It was not until about 1000 hours, after some lengthy fighting in the woods, and with the support of German motorised troops and para-chutists, the support of naval units and the cooperation of the Luftwaffe, that were they able to disengage and reach the Dievenow bridgehead.

Captain Roy's detachment rejoined the *Charlemagne* Battalion at

Dievenow at about 1400 hours and set off with it across Wollin Island towards Kolzow. The battalion reached Swinemünde by short stages. On the way SS-Colonel Zimmermann reported to General Aiching's headquarters at Misdroy, where the chief-of-staff complimented him on the fine bearing of the battalion, marching in orderly ranks and singing, which contrasted so strongly with the general ambiance that the General decided exceptionally to let the battalion retain its arms instead of handing them in, as was customary.

From Swinemünde the battalion set off again for Jargelin, near Anklam, where the Division's other individual escapees were already regrouping, arriving at about noon on 16 March.

Chapter Five

Gotenhafen

Cut off from the rest of the *Charlemagne* Division by the rapid advance of the 3rd Guards Tank Corps on Rummelburg and Köslin, several isolated elements from the fighting at Bärenwalde and Elsenau were unable to follow SS-Major-General Krukenberg's instructions as they passed through Flötenstein to try and rejoin at Greifenberg. Instead they were obliged to withdraw to the northeast, back into the big pocket of Danzig-Gotenhafen with the remains of Colonel-General Walter Weiss's 2nd German Army, which Marshal Rokossovsky's 2nd Byelorussian Front was in the process of reducing.

Consequently, at 0500 hours on 3 March, a detachment commanded by Lieutenant Fatin arrived at Schlawe and met up with Captain René Obitz, who had already gathered together some 300 men from the *Charlemagne*. Soon afterwards a convoy under Captain Jacques Martin arrived at the station, having collected a hundred of the Division's gunners that had completed their training at Josefstadt in Bohemia. At 1600 hours Captain Obitz took over command of the group and chartered a special train that was in the station but without an engine. On the 4th it was learnt that the last railway track to the west had just been cut by the enemy advance near Köslin, thus closing any possible line of retreat by the German 2nd Army.

With no hope of rejoining the depot at Greifenberg or the bulk of the *Charlemagne*, Captain Obitz then placed the French detachment at the disposal of the headquarters of the 4th SS-Police-Panzergrenadier Division, which was commanded by SS-Lieutenant-Colonel Harzer, who had made a name for himself at the battle of Arnhem. The latter directed him to take his group to Neustadt, northeast of Gotenhafen, where the 9th SS-Police Regiment and the 4th SS-Field Training and Replacement Battalion were located.

At about midday on the 5th, the train set off slowly from Schlawe and arrived at Stolp station at about midnight. By chance, at this precise moment a single Russian aircraft dropped three or four bombs that hit the train. As a result, eight men, including Lieutenant Colnion, were killed and sixty wounded, Captain Obitz mortally, and also Lieutenant Salle. According to witnesses, the wagons were running with blood.

Finally, on the evening of the 6th, the train continued its journey to Neustadt carrying the depleted battalion now commanded by Captain Martin with Lieutenant Pierre Fatin as his adjutant and three weak companies commanded by Second Lieutenants Lapard, Bonnefous and Senior Officer-Cadet Jean Chatrousse. Then, next morning, 7 March, Martin and Fatin set off for Danzig to establish contact with an SS headquarters.

Together with Major General Dr Maus' 7th Panzer Division, which had been Rommel's division in 1940, the 4th SS-Police-Panzergrenadier Division formed the IVth Panzer Corps under General Hans von Kessel, but the 7th Panzer Division now only had twenty tanks in working order. The extremely fluid situation was deteriorating by the hour. The Soviets had arrived in front of Neustadt, where they were fortunately stopped by several tanks of the 7th Panzer Division that had been dug in at fixed points for lack of fuel. Encountering this resistance, the enemy wheeled around and enveloped the positions of Martin's battalion, which was without its commander at the time. The detachments of Chatrousse and Lapard succeeded in disengaging themselves and, marching on a rough bearing at night, they found their way to Captain Martin in Danzig.

The battalion no longer had an effective amount of ammunition and was down to one-third of fit, armed men, one-third of unarmed men and one-third of injured, but was still sufficient to

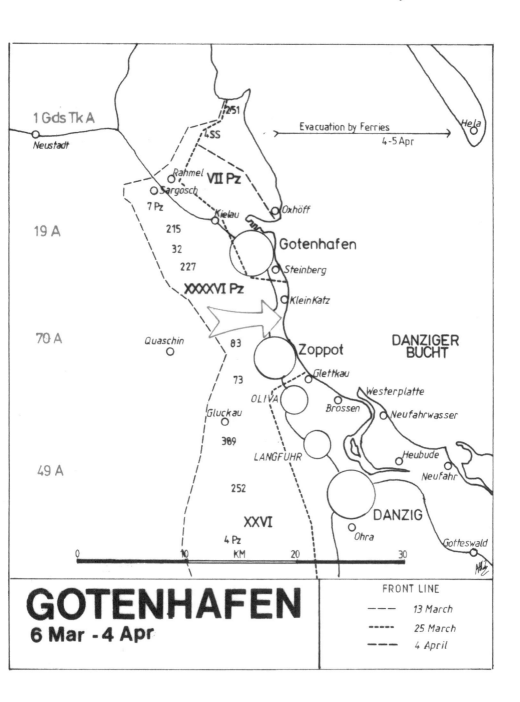

1 Gds Tk A

Neustadt

Evacuation by Ferries
4-5 Apr

Hela

2/51

4 SS

Rahmel

VII Pz

Sargosch

7 Pz

Kielau

Oxhöff

19 A

215

32

227

Gotenhafen

Steinberg

XXXXVI Pz

Klein Katz

70 A

Quaschin

83

Zoppot

DANZIGER
BUCHT

73

Glettkau

OLIVA

Westerplatte

Gluckau

Brossen

Neufahrwasser

389

LANGFUHR

Heubude

49 A

252

Neufahr

XXVI

DANZIG

4 Pz

Ohra

Gotteswald

0   10   KM   20   30

GOTENHAFEN
6 Mar - 4 Apr

FRONT LINE

--- --- 13 March

------ 25 March

— — 4 April

man a third line of defences organised northeast of the important naval installation of Gotenhafen at Kielau, Ciessau and Sagorsch.

The headquarters of the 2nd Army were transferred from Danzig to Pilau in East Prussia and the command of the Gotenhafen pocket given to Lieutenant-General Hans von Kessel's IVth Panzer Corps. This corps, in addition to its organic elements of the 7th Panzer Division and 4th SS-Police Division, also had the remains of the 32nd, 83rd and 203rd Infantry Divisions under command. The IVth Panzer Corps had to stand up to two complete Soviet armies, the 65th and 70th, which were maintaining a constant pressure to annihilate the defenders of the pocket or throw them back into the sea. On 25 March, the 7th Panzer Division withdrew to Oxhöft, and on the 28th the Soviets committed an entire regiment of twenty extra heavy *Josef Stalin* tanks.

Along with the Germans, among the defenders, subjected to bombardments and incessant enemy attacks, and suffering from a lack of water, rations and medical supplies, were French, Latvian, Hungarian, Dutch and Italian troops. Russian propaganda detachments harangued the defenders between pieces of Russian music with loudspeakers calling on them to surrender.

The *Martin* Battalion, now joined by three German NCOs, former members of the French Foreign Legion, was able to stop a Soviet attack, which, after penetrating the first line held by the Germans and driving off the SS Latvians on the second line, failed to breach the French positions, although 160 other Latvians covering the *Martin* Battalion's left flank disappeared in the general confusion.

If they could not be evacuated, the defenders of the pocket were doomed to annihilation. *Reichsführer-SS* Heinrich Himmler agreed to SS-Lieutenant Colonel Harzer's request for permission to evacuate, but this was then refused by Hitler himself. It was entirely due to the efforts of SS-Lieutenant Colonel Harzer, the commander of the 4th SS-Police Division – without the knowledge of Headquarters IVth Panzer Corps, which was adhering to the *Führer-Order* to hold fast – that the defenders of Gotenhafen were eventually evacuated. With an earlier evacuation of technicians and specialists as well as the gun-less artillerymen on 1 April, the *Martin* Battalion was then ferried to the Hela Peninsular when a German squadron arrived, consisting of the cruisers *Lutzow*, *Nurnberg* and *Prinz Eugen* and several destroyers, to give massive fire support as the evacuation continued.

Next day the French succeeded in embarking on a steamship for Denmark, where they disembarked at Copenhagen at 1600 hours on 5 April. After two short stops at Copenhagen and Fredericia, the *Martin* Battalion rejoined the remains of the *Charlemagne* at Neustrelitz in Meckenburg some five days later.

Chapter Six

Reorganisation

Various elements of the *Charlemagne* began assembling near Anklam, only 30km west of Swinemünde. Already present were the officers and about 200 men of the transport column and Divisional service elements that had left Gross Jestin with Russian tanks on their heels at 0200 hours on 4 March.

SS-Major General Krukenberg and the 23 officers and 701 men surviving of the *Fenet* Battalion arrived at about noon on the 16th but, for some inexplicable reason, those who had escaped the siege of Kolberg and had just disembarked at Swinemünd were sent straight to the Replacement Battalion at Wildflecken.

Krukenberg reported to Himmler's field headquarters near Prenzlau on the 18th, returning with a batch of promotions and decorations, including many posthumous awards. Proud of his Frenchmen, Krukenberg was now wearing the *Tricolore* badge on his sleeve.

That same day, SS-Major Katzian was despatched to Wildflecken with orders to return with the Training and Replacement Battalion.

Then on the 21st the troops set off on a four-day march to Neustrelitz in Mecklenburg, there being no trains available. Upon arrival, the Divisional headquarters were established in the village of Carpin, 10km east of the town and the various elements distributed among the surrounding villages.

Orders were then received from SS Headquarters for the reorganisation of the Division by 15 April into a Grenadier Regiment in accordance with the 1945 establishment of two Grenadier Battalions and a Heavy Battalion.

The Divisional units were quartered successively at Bergfeld (Bn 57), Grunow (Bn 58) and Ollendorf (Training Coy) before reaching their specific areas:

Grammerthin	*Charlemagne* Regimental Headquarters (SS-Colonel Zimmermann, later SS-Captain Kroepsch)
Georgenhof	Divisional Combat School (SS-Lieutenant Weber)
Goldenbaum	Heavy Battalion (Captain Boudet-Gheusi)
Fürstensee	57th Battalion (Captain Fenet)
Wokuhl	58th Battalion (SS-Captain Jauss, later SS-Captain Kroepsch)
Drewin	Construction Battalion (Captain Roy)
Zinow	MT and Workshop Section
Thurow	Feldgendarmerie (SS-Lieutenant Görr)
Rodlin	(Lieutenant Fatin)

The Division remained part of Panzer-General Hasso von Manteuffel's 3rd Panzer Army, which, together with the 9th Army, formed Army Group *Weichsel*, now under the command of Colonel-General Gotthardt Heinrici, who had meanwhile taken over from *Reichsführer-SS* Heinrich Himmler.

In expectation of the Russians crossing the Oder, the Division, which was now subordinate to the Rear Area Command with its headquarters at Feldberg, began working on anti-tank defences from 31 March in the area of the lakes east and south of Neustrelitz.

With the Division down to about 700 men, SS-Major-General Krukenberg's first task, was to gather in all his isolated detachments, of which the two most important were those at Wildflecken of regimental size now enlarged by those that had escaped from Kolberg, and the *Martin* Battalion at Gotenhafen, of which there was still no news.

On 27 March, Krukenberg issued the following order of the day:

We have just lived through days interspersed with fighting after some hard marching. We did not fight as a small unit merged within the German Army, but as an autonomous French division. It is with the name *Charlemagne* that the fame for bravery and French determination has been renewed. With pride we recall how we stopped the enemy south of Bärenwalde when he penetrated the German lines. Within an hour we destroyed 16 enemy tanks near Elsenau and Bärenwalde. At Neustettin too we demonstrated our gallantry.

But it was above all at Körlin that we proved that we know how to fight to the last on the field of battle when the rest of the army fled. By holding on until the early hours of the 5th March, we gave part of the German Army and ourselves the chance to get out of the Russian encirclement. We rejoined the German positions near Dievenow after traversing several enemy cordons. It was not only our fighting spirit that gave us success, but also our discipline.

We will not forget our comrades at Kolberg who have been cited several times by the commandant of that fortress for their particularly remarkable bravery. At this very moment, elements of our Division are defending the city of Danzig alongside their German comrades.

Everywhere we have contributed to checking the Bolshevists' breaking wave. This fight could not have taken place without serious losses, but numerous comrades that have succeeded in rejoining our lines. Let us hope that General Puaud will be among those heroic combatants rejoining us soon. Battle has unified us. The fact that our Division has been reduced by glorious battles should incite us again to form only one unit, one team.

So far away from our country, we have been able to surround our flag with a new glory; we know that all Frenchmen, who like us and for the freedom of the country, want a new European order look upon us with pride.

We have always said that the only ones that can take part in restoring France are those who have proved themselves as soldiers under the hardest circumstances. After long months of training, we have been able to show the spirit that animates us, a spirit that in the days to come will lead us to new successes right until the long awaited day when we can participate in the liberation of our country.

History has taught us that after a battle we must not feel fatigue but, on the contrary, gather up all our energy for another fight. The time in which we now live is decisive. Now that we have gained the esteem of the Waffen-SS, no soldier conscious of his honour can leave the ranks.

The glory of the LVF in the east, the success of the French SS-Storm Brigade in the Carpathians, the battles fought by the Militia in our country, should create a unit sealed by the French blood lost in Pomerania and give birth to a tradition worthy of the revolutionary idea for which we are fighting.

Your faith in national-socialist victory is unwavering, even more ferociously if the situation becomes more difficult! Alongside our German comrades fighting for the same ideal, we follow the Führer, liberator of Europe!

More French volunteers continued to arrive to swell the numbers at Carpin, as well as returning wounded and various trainees and specialists that had been detached on various courses, and by early April the *Charlemagne* could muster about 1,000 men. However, there were some serious problems of morale, with contentions between the factions within the ranks, and some lapses in discipline that led to several men being executed by firing squad for offences such as desertion and looting.

Orders for the men of the *Charlemagne* to work on the constructions of field fortifications and anti-tank ditches brought a wave of discontent and the newly promoted Captain Fenet was only able to get his men's cooperation in this matter by setting a personal example.

The LVF marching down
Les Champs-Elysées to an
investiture at Les Invalides
on 27 August 1943.

The LVF parading at Les Invalides for an investiture ceremony
with East Front veterans on the left and a new intake of
volunteers on the right.

The highly decorated RSM
of the LVF.

A recruiting poster for the *Charlemagne*
before that title had been approved.

SS-Major-General Dr Gustav Krukenberg, Commander of the *Charlemagne,* later of the *Nordland*.

Colonel/Brigadier Edgar Puaud, formerly French Foreign Legion, Deputy Commander of the *Charlemagne*.

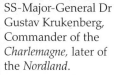

SS-Colonel Walter Zimmermann, Chief Intructor of the *Charlemagne*.

Roman Catholic Padre Count Jean de Mayol de Lupé, here seen with his secretary Henri Caux, volunteered for active service with the LVF at the age of 68 before transferring to the *Charlemagne*, becoming the only padre in the Waffen-SS. Given a six-year prison sentence after the war, he died in prison in 1956.

Major Jean de Vaugelas, ex-French Air Force, Divisional Chief-of-Staff.

Major Paul-Marie Gamory-Dubourdeau, Commander 57th Regiment, later transferred to SS Main Office.

Major Eugène Bridoux, Commander 58th Regiment, resigned December 1944.

Captain Emile Monneuse, First Commander 1st/58th, killed near Belgard.

Captain Victor de Bourmont, First Commander 57th Regiment, missing in action, Pommerania.

Major Boudet-Gheusi, Commander Heavy Battalion after the reorganisation in March 1945.

Captain Henri Josef Fenet, Second Commander 1st/57th and later of the Storm Battalion in Berlin, awarded the Knight's Cross, captured in Berlin.

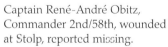

Captain René-André Obitz, Commander 2nd/58th, wounded at Stolp, reported missing.

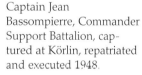

Captain Jean Bassompierre, Commander Support Battalion, captured at Körlin, repatriated and executed 1948.

Captain Berrier, Commander 2nd/58th.

2/Lt Jean Labourdette, Commander 1st Coy, 2nd/58th. Killed in Berlin tunnels.

Sergeant-Major Croiseille, 1st Coy, 2nd/58th.

Lieutenant Pierre Michel, Commander 2nd Coy 2nd/58th. Reported missing in Berlin.

Sergeant-Major Pierre Rostaing, Commander 3 Coy, 2nd/58th.

2/Lt Alfred Brunet, Commander Tank Hunting Unit, awarded Iron Cross First Class.

Officer-Cadet Protopopoff. Killed in Berlin.

Staff-Sergeant Ollivier,
Commander 4th Coy, 2nd/58th.

Sergeant Eugène Vaulot,
awarded Knight's Cross.
Killed in Berlin.

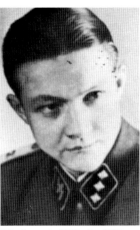

SS-Captain Wilhelm Weber,
Commander Honour
Company, awarded
Knight's Cross.

The Waffen-SS leadership academy at Bad Tölz.

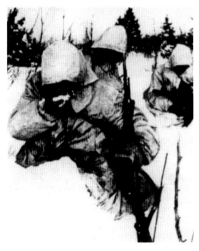

Field conditions in
Pomerania during the
Charlemagne's first
action.

The evacuation of Kolberg under fire.

Lieutenant Fenet manning a machine gun.

The double gates to Hitler's Chancellery on Wilhelmplatz.

Devastation on Friedrichstrasse after the battle.

The U-Bahn entrance at the Kaiserhof Hotel used by Captain Fenet and his party as an escape route.

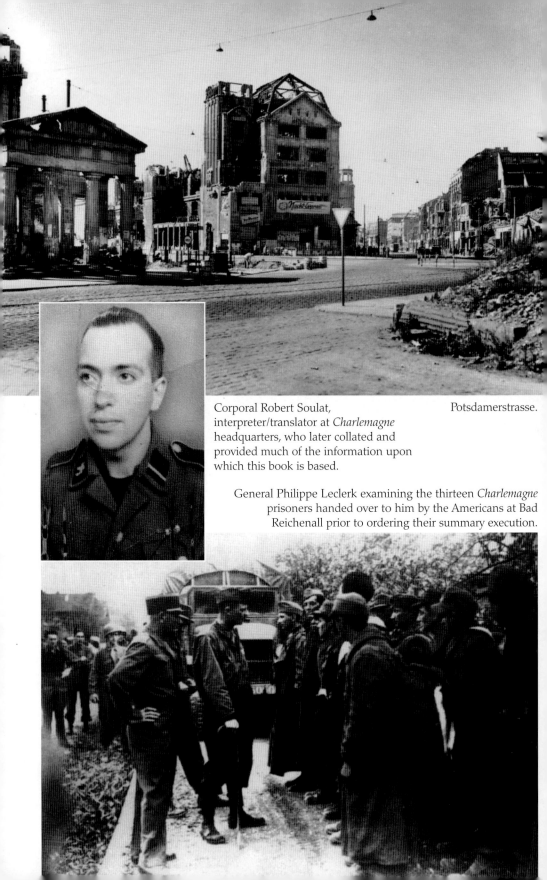

Corporal Robert Soulat,
interpreter/translator at *Charlemagne*
headquarters, who later collated and
provided much of the information upon
which this book is based.

Potsdamerstrasse.

General Philippe Leclerk examining the thirteen *Charlemagne*
prisoners handed over to him by the Americans at Bad
Reichenall prior to ordering their summary execution.

Then *Reichsführer-SS* Heinrich Himmler, in consultation with SS-Major-General Krukenberg, decided that the Division should be reorganised and split into combatant and non-combatant elements. Those who did not wish to fight to the very end would be disarmed and formed into a Construction Battalion. When Krukenberg put this to the troops with words: 'I only want volunteers. You may abandon the armed fight. You will remain in the SS, but as workers. I only want to have combatants with me now.'

One officer and around 400 men, mainly former *Miliciens*, opted for the Construction Battalion, while all of the 80-strong *Compagnie d'Honneur*, some three-quarters of Captain Fenet's Batallion 57, chose to fight on, as did about half of Géromini's Batallion 58. Much against his will, Captain Roy was appointed commander of the Construction Battalion. Géromini, a contentious Corsican character, became a company commander in the Construction Battalion, which was then quartered in the village of Drewin away from the combatant element.

On 10 April the 100 survivors of the Battalion *Martin* rejoined the *Charlemagne* following their adventures at Gotenhafen. Another 1,200 troops under SS-Lieutenant-Colonel Hersche were expected from Wildflecken, which they had left on foot on the night of the 30/31 March. Also expected were the men of the Assault Gun Company that had been training in Bohemia-Moravia, now without their *Hetzers* that had been appropriated by Army Group *Schörner* en route, so they would have to fight as infantry.

Meanwhile, back in France a provisional government had been established under General de Gaulle on 30 August 1944, while Marshal Pétain's Vichy Government had been forcibly removed to Sigmaringen by the Germans, who forbade all contact with the *Charlemagne*. These factors could not be other than a source of constant concern and unrest among the troops with regard to their status and future.

Chapter Seven

Berlin–Neukölln

The story of the *Charlemagne*'s battalion in Berlin is told mainly in the words of their commander and their divisional commander recorded individually several years after the events described.

SS-Major-General Krukenberg recalled:

During the night of Monday 23rd to Tuesday 24th April 1945 at about 0400 hours in the morning I received two telephone calls coming respectively from the Waffen-SS Personnel Office near Fürstenberg and Headquarters Army Group *Weichsel* near Prenzlau, ordering me on behalf of the OKW to go quickly to Berlin and take over command of the 11th SS Panzer Division *Nordland* as a replacement for General Ziegler, who had been relieved on health grounds.

As soon as I arrived in Berlin I was to present myself to General Krebs, the Army Chief of Staff, and to SS-General Fegelein, the Waffen-SS liaison officer, both in the Chancellery.

Because of previous experience, I asked authority to bring with me part of my normal staff and an accompanying detachment of about 90 men. These two requests were agreed by Army Group who laid down the route via Oranienburg and Frohnau as the best way, being still free of the enemy.

I set up the accompanying detachment with volunteers, preferably those with anti-tank experience and gave command of it to Captain Fenet, who had been decorated with the EK I [Iron Cross First Class] and promoted for his conduct in Pomerania. The place and time of departure of the column, two buses and three trucks, was fixed by me for 0830 hours on the 24th April at the southern exit of Alt Steglitz.

This was the same time that Marshal Rokossovsky's army group (2nd Byelorussian Front) launched a new and powerful attack, gaining a foothold on the left bank of the Oder held by Army Group *Weichsel*, to which the Division belonged, pressing a new and last engagement for the *Charlemagne*. Berlin was three-quarters surrounded by the Russian army groups of Zhukov and Koniev, and its impending complete investment boded no delay.

At 0030 hours on the 24th April, I received the order by telegram to form an assault battalion with the remains of the Division and to direct this unit urgently upon Berlin, where I was to present myself at the Chancellery.

This Storm Battalion was formed from three companies of Battalion 57 (plus one from Battalion 58) and reinforced by the divisional combat school (*Compagnie d'Honneur*). The majority of the divisional headquarters also left with the battalion. To counter a lack of heavy weapons, the battalion was mainly equipped with automatic weapons (MG-42 or the assault rifle MP-44) as well as individual anti-tank weapons (*Panzerfausts*). In all probability, the remainder of the battalion would follow next day in second echelon if one could still get through.

The structure of the Storm Battalion was as follows:

Comd: Capt Fenet
Adjt: SS-Lt von Wallenrodt
001:       O/Cdt Frantz
002:       O/Cdt Deuraux
IVb: Lt Dr Herpe
IVd: 2/Lt Abbé Verney

Combat School: SS-Lt Weber
1 Coy/Bn 57:   2/Lt Labourdette
2 Coy/Bn 57:   Lt Michel

3 Coy/Bn 57:	Lt Fatin
4 Coy/Bn 57:	Ssgt Ollivier
6 Coy/Bn 58:	Sgt-Maj Rostaing

Apart from this, I took with me my adjutant, liaison officer, chief medical officer, headquarters commander and several other officers.

At 0500 hours that morning the battalion, about 500 strong, left Carpin by truck for the rendezvous at the southern exit of Neustrelitz.

On its way the column passed an increasing number of vehicles and trucks, whose occupants said that Soviet tanks had been seen not far from Oranienburg. Once could not expect to enter Berlin via Frohnau for much longer. I knew Berlin and its surroundings well from civilian life. I therefore left the north-south route near Löwenberg to head for Neuruppin, reaching the Berlin-Hamburg highway near Friesack. The tracks and roads were crowded with columns of all kinds coming from Berlin.

After coming under air attack at Nauen, we then came under enemy artillery fire near Wustermark. Quitting the main road, we took a lesser road leading to Ketzin. After some six kilometres, we established that isolated enemy groups completing the encirclement of Berlin, and advancing with extreme caution, some coming from the southwest from the direction of Paretz, others from the northeast from the direction of Priort (south of Wustermark), were about to meet up with each other at the exact spot where we were!

We still had to cross the canal near the farms of Falkenrehde, just behind us on the road to Marquardt. If we didn't, the two arrowheads would join up and lose the trap behind us.

As the *Charlemagne* column was about to cross the heavy sandstone bridge, three Voكssturm men mistook us for the enemy and blew the bridge. The vehicles could go no farther

The Southern Suburbs

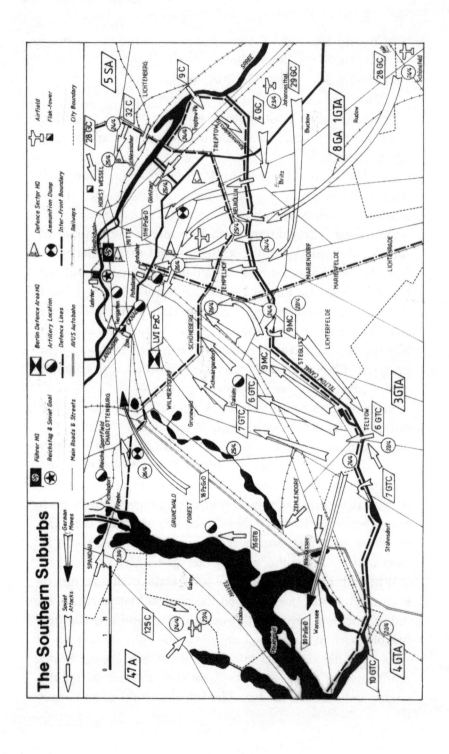

Legend:

Soviet Attacks

German Moves

Reichstag & Soviet Goal

Führer HQ

Berlin Defence Area HQ

Defence Sector HQ

Artillery Location

Ammunition Dump

Airfield

Flak-tower

Main Roads & Streets

Defence Lines

AVUS Autobahn

Inter–Front Boundary

Railways

City Boundary

47 A · 125 C · 5 SA · 28 GC · 32 C · 9 C · LVI PzC · 4 GC · 29 GC · 28 GC · 8 GA · 1 GTA · 9 MC · 3 GTA · 6 GTC · 7 GTC · 10 GTC · 4 GTA

SPANDAU · GATOW · KLADOW · PICHELSDORF · FREYBE · CHARLOTTENBURG · Reich Sport Field · GRUNEWALD FOREST · WILMERSDORF · Grunewald · Schmargendorf · ZEHLENDORF · NIKOLASSEE · Wannsee · STAHNSDORF · TELTOW · LICHTERFELDE · STEGLITZ · SCHÖNEBERG · Dahlem · TEMPELHOF · MARIENFELDE · MARIENDORF · LICHTENRADE · Britz · Buckow · Rudow · SCHÖNEFELD · NEUKÖLLN · TREPTOW · Treptow Pk. · Johannesthal · LICHTENBERG · SPREE · Schlesischer · HORST WESSEL · MITTE · Friedrichstr. · Lehrter · Potsdamer · Anhalter · Tiergarten · Zoo · Landwehr · HAVEL · Pfaueninsel · TEL. SHIP CANAL · TELTOW CANAL

125 C · 18 PzGrD · 20 PzGrD · 55 GTB · 11 PzGrD · Görlitzer · 100 · GCAM

55 GTB

0 1 2 3 M

and would have to turn back. They managed to reach Neustrelitz, but several trucks were lost on the way and three of them returned to Carpin with 90 men, Lieutenants Fatin and Herpe, and Second-Lieutenant Verney.

At 1500 hours on the 24th April, the column that had crossed the canal, now about 300 strong, carried on, having carried across their baggage, mainly ammunition, and reached Pichelsdorf via Marquardt, Glienicke and Gatow without encountering any of the Berlin defence apart from three Hitler Youth armed with Panzerfausts and patrolling on their bicycles. The big bridges across the Havel on the strategic Berlin-Spandau road were barricaded but unguarded!

After a long and fatiguing march on foot of over 20 kilometres, the detachment reached the vicinity of the Reichs Sports Field and camped in the Grunewald Forest not far from the Pichelsdorf Bridge (Freybrücke), which the Soviet artillery was trying to hit. The exhausted men took a rest.

Captain Henri Fenet described the situation:

We reached Berlin in the depth of night, very late, coming in from the west by the last route, where the noose was slowly tightening. The crackling of machine-gun fire now mixed in with the rumbling of artillery from quite close to us. We had been marching for hours, ever since a bridge had been blown from under our feet and made us abandon our trucks. We continued, forcing the pace as the sounds of battle drew closer. Harassed, we marched like automatons, our muscles taunt with the effects of fatigue that we could feel climbing up our legs. We marched on, obsessed by the worry about arriving soon in the encircled capital, of not letting our way be barred from our last battle, all our being, all our strength going towards the goal that attracted us so powerfully: Berlin!

At last we reached it, the last ones were through. Now, stretched out under the pines of the Grunewald we thought of nothing else but sleep, but the din of the Red artillery searching for the Pichelsdorf Bridge (Freybrücke) close by kept us awake.

A violent explosion interrupted the scene. A Red aircraft had come to bring us back to the present. Its bomb landed not far from the bridge and the echo resonated for a long time in the deep valley, but soon silence and calm returned to the black night and we were able to sleep.

Krukenberg continued:

Having confiscated an abandoned vehicle, I left shortly after midnight with SS-Captain Pachur for the Chancellery, where I arrived at about 0030 hours on the 25th April. We waited about three hours in the communications room, from where I was able to inform Army Group *Weichsel* of my arrival.

At about 0330 hours I was introduced to General Krebs, who told me straight-forwardly: 'During these last 48 hours we have ordered numerous officers via the OKW, as well as units outside Berlin, to come immediately to reinforce the defence. You are the first to arrive!'

Generals Krebs and Burgdorf ordered me to report that morning to General of Artillery Weidling, commanding the LVIth Panzer Corps and at the same time 'Commander of the Berlin Defence Area', whose command post was in the offices of the IIIrd Military Region on the Hohenzollern-damm. SS-Lieutenant-General Fegelein could not be found for the moment.

Fenet continued:

When we awoke it was full daylight. The general returned from the Chancellery with a thoughtful expression. Briefly he brought us up to date with the situation and gave us his orders. The encirclement of Berlin had been completed during the night and until now the Russian thrust had been contained in the suburbs, except at Neukölln in the south-east, where there had been some deep penetrations, which had not unduly disturbed the command. It was there, apparently, that we would be engaged.

The general had just been given command of the 11th SS-Volunteer Panzergrenadier Division *Nordland*, to which the French battalion was to be attached as an autonomous unit. The *Nordland* comprised Norwegians, Swedes, and Danes, but was much reduced in strength from the fighting in the winter and early spring, being down to 1,500 effectives.

As the men impatiently watched the Hitler Youth patrols circulating in the Grunewald Forest, our marching orders arrived and were received with pleasure. Our trucks rolled into the city. The loud rumblings of battle came from all around, the furious howling of shells smashing down haphazardly on all parts.

But in this carnival of death, Berlin still maintained an impressive calm. People were walking in the streets as normal, without haste, without panic, functioning normally, content to do so, but with an almost religious gravity.

Krukenberg resumed:

I returned to the Reichs Sport Field at about 0500 hours, then left for the Hohenzollerndamm. Still no sight of the defence forces!

I was received by the chief of staff, Colonel von Dufving, at the command post of the LVIth Panzer Corps, then General Weidling.

The encirclement of the town was completed that night, but the Russians were being held in the suburbs, except in the southeast at Neukölln, where the situation was confused.

It was there that the Division *Nordland* was engaged.

The *Charlemagne* battalion now consisted of the following:

Combat School: SS-Lt Weber
1st Coy: 2/Lt Labourdette
2nd Coy: Lt Michel
3rd Coy: Sgt-Maj Rostaing
4th Coy: Ssgt Ollivier (80 men)

During the afternoon the battalion embarked in trucks in the Grunewald and arrived in Neukölln singing, to the applause of the Berliners.

Once in Berlin the battalion was divided into eight-man sections, each commanded by an energetic NCO and destined to fight in isolation. Two or three of these sections were lead in action by the officers present – Fenet, Weber, etc., but, with these derisory numbers, it was no longer a matter of companies.

Far from being confident, General Weidling, nominated 'Battle Commandant of Berlin' 48 hours beforehand, despite his plans for an active defence, had no more than his own armoured corps, badly mauled in the recent fighting, and his nucleus, the Panzer Division *Müncheberg*, as well as several units such as the 11th SS-Panzergrenadier Division *Nordland*, the Chancellery guards and the Volkssturm, Hitler Youth and several alarm units put together by different organisations, badly trained and inapt in combat.

The southeast of Berlin formed Defence Sector 'C' and had been allocated to the SS-Division *Nordland* by Corps, but its commander, SS-Major-General Ziegler, despite an irreproachable military career, could no longer maintain the cohesion of his scattered troops in the city. He had requested his relief and I had been summoned to Berlin to replace him.

The command post of the *Nordland*, with which all telephone communication had been broken, was situated (at the Pneumology (Lung) Centre opposite the park) on the Hasenheide road between the districts of Kreuzberg and

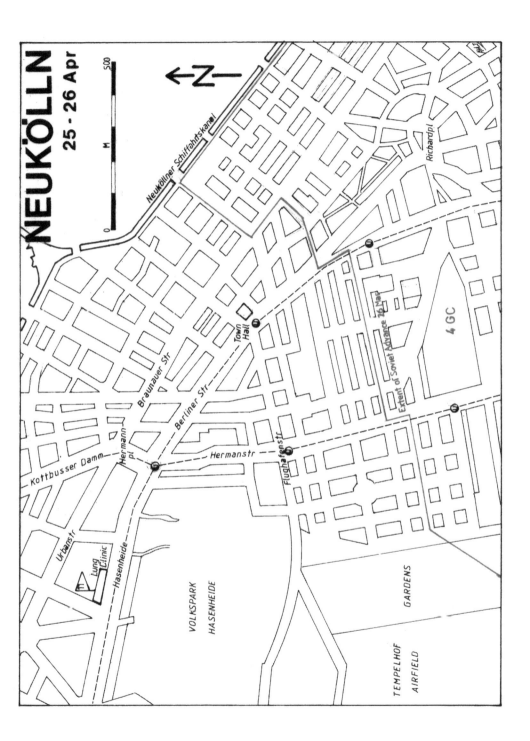

NEUKÖLLN
25 - 26 Apr

N

M
0   500

Neuköllner Schiffahrtskanal

Richardpl.

Town Hall

Braunauer Str

Berliner Str

Extent of Soviet Advance 26 Mar

4 GC

Kottbusser Damm

Hermann pl.

Hermanstr

Flughafenstr

Urbanstr

Lung Clinic

Hasenheide

VOLKSPARK
HASENHEIDE

GARDENS

TEMPELHOF
AIRFIELD

Neukölln. I soon found my way there and found the divisional command post completely disorganised after having been hit by a heavy calibre bomb from a Soviet aircraft.

General Ziegler was waiting to be relieved of his command, and forecast that I would not be able to hold on for more than 48 hours. The defence of Berlin was an impossible task and that was why they were looking for scapegoats in the high places. He had no more than 70 men in the front line. The remainder of the over exhausted troops were returning of their own accord, but his two grenadier regiments, with the exception of the headquarters, could only be considered at most as strong companies or weak battalions.

At noon on the 25th April, SS-Major-General Ziegler handed over the command to me and left for the Chancellery, where I saw him again on the evening of the 1st May.

I sent my liaison officer, SS-Second-Lieutenant Patzak, to get my detachment on alert at the Reichs Sports Field in the *Nordland*'s trucks.

Shortly after Ziegler's departure, two or three armoured personnel carriers arrived from the front filled with wounded, looking for a hospital. Krukenberg's French escorting personnel waiting outside the bunker tried to stop them, and when they failed to stop, one of the Frenchmen opened fire. The co-driver of the leading armoured personnel carrier returned the fire with his machine gun, presumably taking the unknown Frenchmen to be Seydlitz-Troops, wounding three or four of them.

The Division Krukenberg had taken over consisted of only about 1,500 men and 6 self-propelled guns, the divisional artillery having already been deployed in the Tiergarten in the central Corps pool, while the supply and other support elements were located in the Pichelsdorf area.

One of the first orders issued by Krukenberg, who found the organisation so lax, was to restrict movement of subordinate units without prior application for approval in writing. This order, however, only showed his lack of understanding of the current situation on the ground and could not be followed.

Krukenberg continued:

While my adjutant, SS-Captain Pachur reorganised the command post, I set off forward on foot, encountering only Volkssturm, whose chief, a Kreisleiter, had set up his command post at Hermannplatz in a big building on the corner of Hasenheide and the Kottbusser Damm (the Karstadt Department Store), from the first floor of which he had an overall view.

According to him, the Soviets coming from the east had occupied Treptow District the day before. Previously he had posted some weak outposts as far as the Urbandamm and at Sonnenallee, but he could not count on them putting up a resistance, as they only had a few machine guns and very little ammunition. To his left he had public telephone communication with the Görlitzer Railway Station sector, whose chief, Reichsleiter Hilgenfeld, had fallen two hours previously.

After a restful night, despite an aerial bombardment close to Hasenheide, Fenets's battalion set off at daybreak on the 26th April,for Neukölln town hall, where they were supposed to assist with a counterattack by the *Nordland* at 0500 hours. In fact the attack, supported by several tanks and self-propelled guns did not start until 0600 hours.

Right at the outset, while Ssgt Ollivier, commanding the 4th Company, which had been given a support task, was giving orders to his section leaders gathered around him, the company was taken by surprise by a Russian anti-tank gun. Seventeen men were killed with one blow and the numerous wounded including Ollivier and SS-WO II Fieselbrand, a section commander. officer-cadet Protopopoff assumed command of the 4th Company while the wounded were evacuated.

Captain Fenet gave his account of the action:

We held an arms inspection not far from Hasenheide Park. At
0500 hours next day we were to go into the attack with other
Nordland units and chase the Reds out of Neukölln. As night
fell, we set up sentry posts at the crossroads. The night was
strangely calm as we went about the dark and deserted
streets, the only sound being the crunching of glass shards
under our boots. The Neukölln Canal (Neuköllner
Schiffahrtskanal) gave us some anxiety, but that too was calm
with its bridges, quays and sleeping black water. A humming
sound comes through the air. Aircraft! The district was
shaken for hours by the uninterrupted din of explosions that
made the ground tremble and cracked the walls. Would the
Reds use this deluge as cover for a night attack? Our sentries
were alerted, but the Reds still did not budge that night, and
after the crash of the last bombs, silence fell once more.

The companies assembled for the attack before daybreak
and the columns set off in silence towards the town hall, from
where the attack was to begin. The tanks were already there.
On the corner of the street, an enormous *Königstiger*, massive
on its wide tracks, extended its interminable 88mm gun, and
there were some *Panthers* a bit further back with their fine
silhouettes, then the *Sturmgeschütze*, assault guns with squat
70mm barrels. Their crews were quietly awaiting the
departure time, a little as if they were going for a drive. We
discussed the plan of attack down to minute detail. The
grenadiers would advance alongside the armour, clearing the
buildings and side-streets, and covering the tanks, which in
turn would provide covering fire.

0500 hours. Nothing moves. The divisional attack is still
not ready. 0530 hours, still nothing. Usually we do not pay
much attention to such annoyances, but today this worries us.
Finally, a little before 0600 hours, the order to set off arrives.
The infantry advance well spaced out, followed by the tanks.

The Reds fail to react for a few moments, but then their old Maxim machine guns open up with their slow and steady rhythm, followed by the anti-tank guns, which salute us with their angry barks. Our men advance as if on exercise, bounding from door to door along the walls, jumping or scrambling over the ruins, dodging the Red snipers firing from above. The tanks behind us spit fire and flames, their intervention visibly disquieting the opposition, who turn to the defensive. Their infantry only reveal themselves as apparently isolated snipers and leave the heavy arms, machine guns, anti-tank guns and mortars to hose us down. However, the enemy's violent fire does not prevent the regular advance of the grenadiers, who continue to bound forward nimbly and quickly.

We suffer a severe blow, however. A reserve section is about to negotiate a crossroads near the town hall, believing itself under cover, imprudently bunched, when a salvo of anti-tank gun shells hit the street corner with terrible precision, riddling the unfortunate men, smashing them to the pavement or against the surrounding walls. Broken hearted, I counted 15 bodies scattered on the roadway.

Meanwhile, the volunteers continued to advance, despite strong Soviet resistance. It was now necessary to clear building after building with grenades and bayonets. All along the streets leading to the town hall one could see men reappear as they moved in bounds, arriving in bursts at the command post to refill their haversacks and pockets with ammunition, and leaving again with the same agility under the admiring eyes of the Berliners, who watched the combative ardour of the French with admiration. In practically every building one saw old men and women emerging from their cellars to find out what was happening and to see for themselves. We told them that the aim of our attack that morning was to clear the enemy out of Neukölln. 'May you succeed', they told us, hoping that the Reds would get to them. Often they came up to us with a cup of coffee or a glass of water in their hands. 'Drink up; you must be thirsty!' Others insisted that we spend a few minutes with them in their cellars to share a meal prepared from the last of their rations. All this was very kind and very moving, but we really had to get on with the job.

However, as our men advanced, liaison with units on either side became precarious. On the right and left the situation appeared quite confused, and already there was a threat to our flanks as we reduced the enemy wedge in our lines, and we had to regain contact with the units to the left and right that were still preventing the wedge from expanding. But it seemed that there was no one there but Russians. Then an order arrived from Division: 'If the attack has not started, stop and await new orders. If not, do your best!'

What did it mean? What was happening? SS-Lieutenant Joachim von Wallenrodt, the adjutant, immediately set off for Division and returned much later with the required orders. It was bad. We were the only unit to have attacked. That morning, the 26th April, at the same time as we set off from the town hall, the Reds had unleashed the floodgates of their formidable forces on Berlin. Already the capital's defensive belt was beginning to crack a little everywhere.

'Just our luck!' I said to von Wallenrodt, 'we have just taken half a district from Ivan, and now we have to abandon it, just like Heinrichswalde two months ago! Three hours after our attack we had to quit because there was no longer any front behind or alongside us. It was infuriating!'

'What shall we do, Captain?' asked von Wallenrodt phlegmatically.

'Assuredly we stay here. Should the situation stabilise itself on the flanks, we can hold on to what we have won, and if it gets worse, we shall see. For the moment we remain, and won't let ourselves be surrounded.'

We now formed a salient within the Russian lines and

progressively I had to reduce the numbers at the head in order to reinforce the flanks. The town hall became the centre of our defence and we concentrated most our forces there. We had already received reinforcement in the form of a *Bann* of Hitler Youth, several hundred boys of between fourteen and sixteen yeas of age, who charged with a magnificent spirit, blind and deaf to danger, uncaringly throwing themselves at the enemy, strong in their juvenile inexperience! Moreover, these youngsters fought like old soldiers! On preceding days we had seen them leaving in commandos into the suburbs to neutralise the advancing tanks, today we find them again in the street fighting alongside us, the most savage, the hardest, most murderous possible. They go ahead with their *Panzerfausts*, with rifles often taller than themselves, as naturally as if they were marching with a brass band and drums, unconcerned about their losses however numerous, and clearly aiming to perform as well as their elders.

Since morning the Reds have suffered heavy losses. Tanks and grenadiers have destroyed about 30 tanks, while the Red infantry, which has been reinforced by the hour, has left numerous dead and wounded on the ground, and several anti-tank guns have been knocked out. The fighting continues relentlessly.

The battalion runners tore along through the ruins, across streets swept by blasts and explosions to maintain contact with the attacking companies. Their leader, Corporal Millet, 20 years old, naturally took on the more important and more dangerous tasks. More than once since this morning we thought that we would never see him again, but always he returned, cool and calm: 'Mission accomplished.' During the afternoon we made a tour of all the units then returned to the town hall, on which the Reds seem to want to make a big effort by taking us in the flank.

At the moment that we enter the street to re-enter the town

hall there is an explosion. Millet doubled up and fell face down, a last tremor and then he lay still. The enemy barrage continued to sweep the street and I felt a sharp pain in my left foot. I found myself without knowing how in the entrance to the town hall, from where I was taken inside. The barrage continued to fall outside. There was no time to lose, the Reds were much closer than we had thought. They were behind us, perhaps 50 metres from the town hall. Immediately, I had this dangerous sector swept clean, hobbling and cursing, because I now needed a stick and an assistant to walk. This is a fine time to get a bullet through the foot!

After some furious fighting, man to man with bayonet duels, throwing grenades from door to door and window to window, the Reds who had tried to take us in the rear were wiped out or fled. But, following the check of this attempt, they now tried to launch a frontal attack, and this time they spared neither their fire nor their men. We had no intention of letting them get away with this. Our men and the Hitler Youth installed in the town hall fought like devils, taking advantage of a moment when the Reds seemed to hesitate and made a sortie in strength that dislocated their move completely and enabled us to clear the area.

Most of this fighting took place inside blocks of buildings, but now the tanks joined in, and T-34s arrived head to tail. Our *Panzerfausts* destroyed one or two, but the others continued on their way. Alerted, the *Königstiger* set up an ambush in a side-street and waited. Not far from it, I followed the sound of the Red tanks with my ears; the noise of the tank tracks got nearer, and I could hear their engines. They were quite close. The long 88mm barrel of the *Königstiger* lowered slowly, the front of the first T-34 appears, then its turret. There was a dry, violent explosion and flames and smoke surged out of the muzzle brake of the 88mm gun, which recoiled sharply, leaving the T-34 neatly immobilised. Our men covered the hatch with their rifles, but it didn't open. With a direct hit on the turret, the T–34 was dead, completely dead.

Millet was still there, stretched out on the pavement in his camouflage tunic of brown and green dots, his blond hair dirty with dust, his red face already dulled in death. The barrage had caught him in the side and he had been killed instantly. His comrades carried his body into shelter.

Roger, 19, a big devil with black hair, a cold aspect and a fanatical soul, took his place. He enlisted at the age of 17, and to the officer who said to him a little mockingly: 'Our kind of life is much too hard for the French,' he replied tit for tat: 'Not for everyone, and that is precisely why I am enlisting!'

He has already taken part in two campaigns without getting a scratch, but the trip to Berlin started off badly for him. The day before yesterday when the bridge was blown up in front of us, he was blown into the canal below. Completely blinded, his eyes full of dirt, he had only recovered his sight the day before.

As the afternoon progressed, our situation at the town hall became more critical. With the front line yielded back on both sides, we no longer had any neighbours and there did not seem to be much behind us. We could only hold our position through the extraordinary dynamism of our men. Cap, the little Flemish sergeant, had grabbed a machine gun and was holding a street on his own. At a rate of 1,200 rounds a minute, he was hosing down anything that moved in front of him with a precision and rapid reflex of action that visibly disconcerts the Reds. From time to time he made a rapid change of position, going behind another bit of wall, another heap of rubble, and resumed harassing the assailants. Fink, who was acting as my crutch, requisitioned a Hitler Youth in passing for this role, which was too placid for his taste, and went to rejoin Cap: 'Let me take over for a bit, you're going to kill yourself!' Relieving each other from time to time, they held the street until the evening without the Reds being able to advance a metre.

For five hours we had been completely alone in front of the lines. The few tanks that still had fuel and ammunition remained with us, while the others pulled back. Cut off from the Division, we decided to stay in the town hall as long as a line of retreat remained to our lines. The Reds could cut off our retreat with 50 men, but no doubt they would not dream of it and tried desperately to attack us from the front or sides with their tanks supported by several hundred men. A wasted effort; the tanks burst into flames or had to turn back, and the infantry bit the dust as soon as they dared expose themselves. There was now an infernal din, the shelling being nourished from one place or another and we could no longer distinguish between it increasing or dwindling. At each street corner one was regularly shaken by an explosion, covered in dust, eardrums aching. If one was lucky, it was just one of our hidden tanks that had just fired, but it was more likely to be a volley from the Ivans opposite.

Towards 1900 hours the battalion runners reported that Red tanks had reached Hermannplatz, 900 metres behind us. Only two streets remained free and, no doubt, not for much longer. This time we had to leave, for once Hermannplatz was blocked, there would be no way out. I used a pause in the fighting to regroup the Hitler Youth and SS, and we pulled back with the tanks without the Reds trying to stop us. We reached Hermannplatz a little later without difficulty and found the defence there being hastily organised behind barricades of paving stones. We were just in time: the T-34s were keeping a respectful distance of several hundred yards and, several minutes after our arrival, all the arteries leading from the square to the east were in enemy hands.

The assault guns stayed close to us and started a veritable massacre of Russian tanks as they tried to encroach on the square. A bull's eye and the dusk was illuminated with the light of all these tanks in flames, exposing one after another to a great din. The battle continued well into the night, but the Red infantry did not show themselves.

At about midnight the order came for us to withdraw. On the way we were rejoined by Labourdette and his No. 1 Company, which had remained at the disposal of the Division all day and had had to intervene to parry enemy infiltrations when the front gave way. Labourdette told me that he had just been requisitioned by the Defence Sector commander, whom he does not come under, to seal a new breach. That was none of my business, but after the long day we have just been through, I was relying on No. 1 Company, the only fresh unit remaining in the battalion, to make up my losses. I explained this to the Defence Sector commander, requesting he should at least let the last survivors of the French Division fight on together! I used the occasion to tell him of my surprise to find the defence organised in such a desultory fashion.

Naively, I thought that the belt defence of Berlin would be formed from regular units organised like ourselves and I could not understand how the front had cracked so quickly, because in our sector we had held and would have continued holding much longer had it not been for the total absence of neighbours having allowed the Reds to encircle us. It was the turn of the person with whom I was talking to be astonished at my astonishment. If all the Berlin front was as well off for troops as our sector, we would not now be behind Hermannplatz! In fact, of properly constituted units, there were only the remains of General Weidling's armoured corps and some SS units, which included our battalion, the *Nordland* Division and some *Leibstandarte Adolf Hitler* troops at the Reichs Chancellery, not amounting to more than 2–3,000 men when the battle began! Most of the troops were in hastily-formed ad hoc units of Hitler Youth, Volkssturm and over-age policemen. All were of good will, many, especially the Hitler Youth, were fighting magnificently, but this was not enough. Cadres were lacking, there was no artillery, hardly any tanks, fuel and ammunition was strictly rationed.

Meanwhile the situation was becoming catastrophic in our sector and, in view of the urgency, I agreed for No. 1 Company to take part in a limited operation while the rest of the battalion took several hours' rest.

Before leaving, I recommended to Labourdette that he should not let himself become involved and to return at all costs at the agreed time. 'You can count on me,' he replied, but in hearing him I sensed a painful presentiment. I took him by the shoulder: 'You must return with the lads, you must return yourself, do you understand?'

There was a brief silence. 'Don't worry, I'll be back,' he said in a distant voice and a little hesitantly, as if the words were refusing to come out.

'Right, see you soon!'

'See you soon, Captain.'

We shook hands and he disappeared into the night with his men. I watched his silhouette fade with a pang of anguish. His attitude disturbed me. It was that of a man going into battle knowing that he would not return. But no, this was ridiculous. I shrugged my shoulders, furious with myself for letting myself think that way. My nerves were on edge, no doubt, and the fault lay with the ridiculous wound which made me walk with crutches. No, Labourdette would return. That winter he had magnificently won under fire the insignia of a Second-Lieutenant, for which the officer-cadet school had considered him too timid, having decided last autumn to go through the course once more. Timid, he certainly had been, but since Pomerania that was over. Prolonged contact with the Reds had given him confidence.

Roger interrupted my thoughts by bringing me a chair and urging me to rest. 'Not now, Roger!' Right now I had to find somewhere for my men to sleep for a few hours. Von

Wallenrodt, who had gone off to search, had found room in the Thomas Keller opposite the Anhalter Railway Station. He would lead the battalion there and we were to meet later in the morning at the Divisional command post, which I wanted to get back to straight away. Von Wallenrodt set off with the men, while Officer-Cadet Douroux and myself vainly searched for a vehicle to take us into the city centre. The command post of one of the *Nordland* regiments was quite close, and there we learned that there was not a drop of petrol available at the moment, and also that the general was about to move again, but no one knew where. While waiting, we were invited to use the time to sleep in the shelter, which was also serving as a dressing station.

SS-Major-General Krukenberg noted that since the morning, the tanks and grenadiers had destroyed thirty enemy tanks and several anti-tank guns, apart from inflicting heavy casualties on the Russian infantry. His account continued:

Towards the end of the morning of the 26th, Staff-Sergeant Ollivier left the ambulance near the Tiergarten and set off to find the Fenet Battalion to resume command of the 4th Company, when he came face to face with SS-Captain Heller, an instructor at the Breslau Infantry Gun School, where he had done a course with the 10th Company of the 57th Battalion. He was immediately commandeered to command a section of two 150mm infantry guns served by recruits of the SS-Division *Das Reich*, two SS-corporals performing the combined roles of gun team leaders and aimers. With great difficulty, these two guns were finally deployed on an avenue controlling an important crossroads 500 metres away. The first tank appeared at the end of a quarter of an hour and was destroyed by a shot to the rear, and eight others received the same fate. But it was impossible to camouflage and difficult to redeploy, and a volley from

Stalin Organs wiped out the first gun with its truck and team. Redeployed in a small parallel street, the second gun succeeded in expending all its ammunition.

Having remained until 1700 hours in a laundry used as a command post by the Heller section, Staff-Sergeant Ollivier suddenly saw SS-Lieutenant von Wallenrodt of the division enter, who then took him back to the Fenet Battalion near the Opera, where he resumed command of the 4th Company, now reduced to 20 men under officer-cadet Protopopoff. During the course of the 27th, the latter had succeeded in shooting down a Russian reconnaissance aircraft with a machine gun. There were several encounters with Russian patrols without loss.

The damage caused by the aerial bombing was so serious that it was impossible to command from this position. I therefore asked and obtained permission from Corps, which had meanwhile moved from the Hohenzollerndamm to Bendlerstrasse, to transfer my command post to Gneisenau Police Barracks, also requesting being absolved from responsibility for Sector 'C' and that I be allocated a more central zone for the *Nordland*. At the same time I also signalled the presence of two police battalions in the barracks, perfectly equipped and rested, and completely forgotten about, that were quite capable of holding the sector in place of the *Nordland*, which was now in the need of a complete overhaul. The *Nordland* was assigned to the Gendarmenmarkt area and I provisionally selected the cellars of the Opera house for my command post.

Chapter Eight

Berlin–Mitte

SS-Major-General Krukenberg continued his account:

At about 2000 hours I returned to the Corps command post to get my instructions for our future employment. There the chief of staff gave me the orders to engage the *Nordland* next day in the central Defence Sector 'Z', whose commander was a Luftwaffe-Lieutenant-Colonel Seifert with his command post in the Air Ministry.

I immediately went to the Air Ministry, where I was received by Lieutenant-Colonel Seifert in the presence of his liaison officer, who constituted his whole staff! Straight away he told me that he had no need of my regimental commanders, or their staffs, because the effectives of their respective units did not amount to more than a single battalion. I retorted that more grenadiers were rejoining every day, that they were Scandinavian volunteers confident in their normal superiors and that it would be dangerous to separate them in the present situation. Moreover, Sector 'Z' would become the core of the defence. The more one deployed experienced officers the greater would be the strength of the resistance.

Lieutenant-Colonel Seifert refuted my argument and told me that in his sector everything had been prepared in such a way that we would not need any support. He showed me a map on which were featured command posts, machine-gun nests and other combat positions. When I finally asked him if he would like to have one or two of those accompanying me to reinforce his command post, he refused in an arrogant manner. He would not change his mind, even when in order to overcome his prejudice, I told him that I had only been with Waffen-SS for a year and that during the First World War I had served in Army Headquarters. He dodged my question about what had already been done in this sector, saying that everything was being organised.

I returned to my command post in the Opera most annoyed. After a short rest, I informed the commanders of the Regiments *Danmark* and *Norge* about the orders from Corps and the attitude of Lieutenant-Colonel Seifert, asking them to use the next morning to reassemble their units and put them into order.

It should be noted here that, although Seifert had been appointed Defence Sector commander of this central sector that included the Reichs Chancellery, SS-General Wilhelm Mohnke was responsible for the defence of the Reichs Chancellery and regarded all SS troops in the immediate area as subordinate to him, a situation that only added to the general confusion at this stage of the battle.

27 April
Krukenberg continued:

The night of the 26th–27th April passed without disturbance. Next morning was passed in reorganising and re-supplying the troops. Towards midday the commanders of the *Norge* and *Danmark* reported that each of the two regiments disposed anew of an effective strength of between 6–700 men. I gave orders that not more than a third were to be placed at the disposition of Sector Headquarters and to continue to prepare the remainder for battle. At the same time I ordered that even if Sector Headquarters did not want to speak to them, the commanders remained responsible for their troops and that during the afternoon they should make

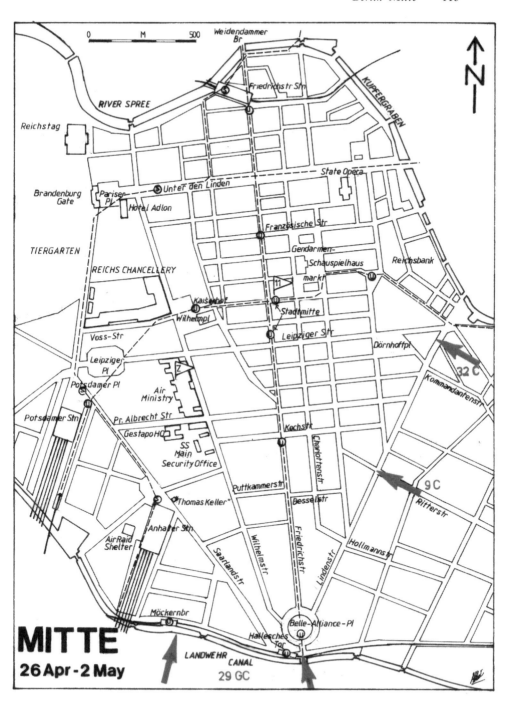

MITTE

26 Apr - 2 May

themselves familiar in advance with the conditions in which their troops would have to fight.

Towards 1900 hours, the commanders signalled that they had found no one behind our grenadiers and that nowhere had they been able to discover the command posts or machine-gun nests that I had indicated as ready. With that I had the impression that all the defensive plans of Sector 'Z' existed only on paper and began to realise why my offers of assistance had been refused.

I decided not to defer any longer presenting myself to the Waffen-SS liaison officer to the Führer, SS-General Fegelein, and to go myself. Describing to him what had happened, I begged him to support me in my efforts to prevent the dissipation of the only SS division in the Berlin Defence Area. Defence Sector 'Z', where it was to be engaged, would become in time of capital importance. So far its preparations existed only on paper! There would be serious consequences if the regimental commanders of the *Nordland* were to be removed, having already removed their divisional commander, SS-Major-General Ziegler, whom they fully trusted. It would then be easy to blame the Waffen-SS for any setback in the defence of Sector 'Z'.

I repeated all my objections to General Weidling, who entered the room at that moment, begging him, to his obvious annoyance, to engage the only experienced formation in the city centre under the command of its own officers. In any case, he wanted to leave Lieutenant-Colonel Seifert only the sector immediately leading to the Chancellery.

Eventually he aquiesced in subordinating the whole of Sector 'Z' to SS-General Mohnke, commander of the Chancellery, and in forming two sub-sectors: that on the right with its command post in the Air Ministry reserved for Lieutenant-Colonel Seifert. Outside the boundary formed by the centre of Wilhelmstrasse the *Nordland* would be engaged under its own officers, its sector being limited on the east side by Döhnhoffplatz–Kommandantenstrasse–Alexandrinenstrasse.

Stadtmitte U-Bahn Station was nominated as the city centre command post. The *Nordland* units already engaged in Seifert's sector would stay there until relieved by others and then return to my control. General Weidling then left and I never saw him again nor received any further orders from him.

It was already 0100 hours on the morning of the 27th April when I returned to the Opera.

Meanwhile, the majority of the French volunteers of the Storm Battalion were sat, half-asleep in the entrance of a block of flats on Belle-Alliance-Platz. These troops were the remnants of only three of the companies. The 2nd Company was effectively reduced to the strength of a section, its Company Commander, Lieutenant Pierre Michel, having been gravely wounded the previous evening. The 3rd Company was down to Sergeant-Major Pierre Rostaing with twenty-five men, all the section leaders and many of the men having been either killed or wounded in Neukölln. The 4th Company was temporarily commanded by Officer-Cadet Serge Protopopoff in the absence of Staff-Sergeant Jean Ollivier, and had had one section completely wiped out the previous day.

Detached from the battalion, the 1st Company, commanded by Second-Lieutenant Jean Labourdette, had been engaged the previous day further west, to the north of Tempelhof Airport. One of its platoons had been engaged defending the Landwehr Canal near the Hallesche Tor while attached to a unit commanded by the signals officer of the 2nd Battalion, SS-Panzergrenadier Regiment 24 *Danmark*, SS-Second-Lieutenant Bachmann, facing attacks from Soviet armour, shelling and mortar fire.

Meanwhile, the SS-Lieutenant Weber's Combat School had gone off in the direction of the Reichs Chancellery.

At 0500 hours the 1st Company rejoined the remains of the battalion to the relief of Captain Henri Fenet, who now had to negotiate with Lieutenant-Colonel Seifert, who wanted these men to reinforce his poorly manned sector. A section was sent off to the north, but was almost immediately eliminated by a shell-burst, which killed two men and badly wounded the other three.

The battalion adjutant, SS-Lieutenant Joachim von Wallenrodt, found accommodation for the battalion in the Thomas Keller pub opposite the Anhalter railway station, several hundred metres to the northwest, where the men were able to stretch themselves out on the tables and benches for several hours of sleep.

Meanwhile, Captain Fenet was accompanied and supported by his liaision officer, Officer-Cadet Alfred Douroux, for Fenet had been wounded in the foot by a machine-gun bullet. The pain was such that they stopped at the Regiment *Danmark*'s first-aid post in the cellars of the Reichsbank, where Fenet rested for several hours in a state of semi-consciousness. At daybreak an elderly Wehrmacht officer helped him on to the *Nordland*'s headquarters, which had been installed in the cellars of the Opera House since the 25th, and where SS-Major-General Krukenberg was holding a command conference. He told Fenet that he was very pleased with the work of the French battalion and that they would have the whole of the day off before reorganising into eight-man tank-destroying sections in support of the armour and assault guns based on Leipziger Strasse.

Krukenberg continued:

During the morning I returned to the Chancellery once more to introduce myself to the new sector commander, SS-General Mohnke, but met General Krebs, who told me that the advance guard of General Wenck's army had just reached Werder, west of Potsdam. He knew nothing new about the state of negotiations with the West, but the Americans were certainly in a position to cover the 90 kilometres between the Elbe and Berlin in very little time and restore the situation in the city.

During my visit, SS-General Mohnke promised to give me

all the support possible in my difficult task and told me that he would place at my disposal a company of sailors that had flown in during the night and were in the Ministry of Foreign Affairs garden. Moreover, the Nordland's SS 503rd Heavy Tank Battalion, which still had eight tanks and self-propelled guns, would remain under my command. These two trumps reinforced our defensive capability.

On the 27th April the situation was calm within the formation and only a few individual Russian soldiers tried to advance cautiously along Blücherstrasse towards the canal at the Hallesche Tor.

Captain Henri Fenet continued his account:

All morning the shells continued to crash down on the Opera House, Schloss Berlin and the surrounding area with such violence that the headquarters moved to a less unpleasant place as soon as there was a gap in the shelling. This was at the Schauspielhaus (now Konzerthaus) and then in Stadtmitte U-Bahn Station. On the way, the medical officer said that we were on Französische Strasse (French Street). Two and a half centuries ago our Hugenot ancestors had installed themselves in the area we were about to defend.

Shortly afterwards von Wallenrodt collected the battalion and the general proceeded to award Iron Crosses won the previous day in his underground command post. We were very happy to be together again and this break of several hours had been most welcome for us all. The men gathered around me bustled around, filling my pockets with sweets, chocolates and cigarettes that they had just been given. They sang happily in the underground carriages, but the party was incomplete, for No. 1 Company was still missing. What the hell had happened to Labourdette?

It was only towards the end of the afternoon that de Lacaze, an Officer-Cadet in the 1st Company, arrived with the bulk of the effectives. Labourdette was not among them. He had left with several of his men for an outer position in the U-Bahn tunnels while giving de Lacaze orders not to worry about him but to gather up the rest of the company at the stipulated time should he not have returned, in which case he should go straight to the command post. He had not been seen since. At the last contact, he had not been at the location where he had set himself up in a primitive fashion, and it had not been possible to trace him. We were not particularly worried for the moment, for in these battle conditions several hours of delay were nothing extraordinary, but it was not much later that we learned of Labourdette's death. He had fallen in the tunnels, riddled with bullets while returning from a reconnaissance and protecting the withdrawal of his men with an assault rifle. He was 22 years old and immensely proud of having been enlisted as No. 3 in the French SS.

Krukenberg continued:

Meanwhile, the 1st Company under Second-Lieutenant Labourdette was engaged in a sector better prepared with dug-in tanks and solid barricades. de Lacaze's platoon was engaged in defending one of these, whilst Croisile's platoon, reduced to 20 men, deployed in the U-Bahn to counter eventual underground probes. When they came up again, de Lacaze's platoon had disappeared. During a bombardment that followed, the platoon gathered in a small group under Officer-Cadet Robelin. There were a few casualties.

Towards midday, the company was taken over by a Wehrmacht major near Yorckstrasse S-Bahn Station. T-34 tanks were swarming about to the east. The S-Bahn bridges (over Yorckstrasse) were blown and dropped into the street. There they encountered a young French civilian whose only concern was to know how he could get back to the little factory in the area where he worked!

The company took shelter under a porch while awaiting a counterattack. Robelin left with his platoon to rejoin the Fenet Battalion, but they were never seen again. Croisile's platoon was down to 14 men, plus a Wehrmacht soldier, one airman and one Volkssturm man. Only one machine gun in firing condition remained, but they had assault rifles.

At about 1400 hours a small counterattack to enable the major to evacuate his wounded succeeded. Seven tanks arrived via Yorckstrasse and the Russians came from every-where, but hesitated tackling a group so strong. Five or six disguised as civilians and pulling a cart were fired on and fled. An old gentlemen politely asked Labourdette to remove boxes of ammunition stacked in his apartment on the 5th floor. When they were opened, they were found to contain *Panzerfausts*. What a windfall! The first T-34 to approach was missed by Croisile, but hit by the Wehrmacht soldier. However, news was scarce and uncertain, and couriers often failed to return.

Meanwhile the Sub-Sector *Stadtmitte* was occupied without incident and lookouts were posted along the Landwehr Canal. On the wings, the Regiments *Danmark* and *Norge* had a third of their effectives in lines in the rubble south of Hollmannstrasse. In the event of an attack in force, they were to withdraw slowly to the principal line of resis-tance on the level of Besselstrasse and Ritterstrasse, where prepared nests of anti-tank and machine guns would offer them the necessary support.

At their command post level, the battalions and regiments held a third of their grenadiers formed into shock troops ready to move forward quickly by passages pierced through the buildings to reject any enemy that penetrated our lines.

A last third, held in relative rest in Leipziger Strasse, was to stay there. This street, just about suitable for traffic, served as a deployment route for our tanks, which were supported by groups of tank-hunting detachments of French volunteers. The remainder of the latter and the Engineer Company of the *Nordland* remained in the cellars of the Opera or the Allianz building, from where they could easily join them.

The integral occupation of Sub-Sector *Stadtmitte* failed primarily because at the beginning Lieutenant Colonel Seifert only released those elements that had been placed at his disposal slowly.

Apart from this, various groups of reinforcements continued to join us, particularly SS volunteers so that soon the whole of Europe was represented. (Among these reinforcements was a company of naval radar trainees that had been flown in and were armed with Italian rifles but had received no infantry training.) These elements remained behind the Sector wings to prevent any surprise attacks from neighbouring sectors.

As for artillery, this was assembled out of sight of aerial view in the Tiergarten under the orders of Colonel Wöhlermann, artillery chief of the LVIth Panzer Corps, because no plans had been made for its deployment in the defence. I had the guns deployed behind our Sector at the entrance of streets leading on to the Unter den Linden, so that they could at least check any tanks surging in from the north, from the Reichstag or Schlossplatz because, despite repeated enquiries, the situation remained obscure for us.

That afternoon I went to the command post assigned to me by General Weidling, an abandoned U-Bahn wagon with broken windows, no electricity or telephone, in Stadtmitte U-Bahn station. Such was the command post of the *Stadtmitte* Sector in the Berlin fortress!

The vault of the station was soon pierced by a medium shell that caused us 15 wounded evacuated to the first aid post organised by the *Nordland*'s senior medical officer, Colonel Dr Zimmermann, in the air raid shelter of the Hotel Adlon on Pariser Platz.

Captain Fenet was in the command post when this occurred:

News was received of the outside. The Wenck Army, which was trying to reach the capital, had reached the outskirts of Potsdam. On the other hand, the Reds had launched their big offensive across the Oder that we had been expecting for weeks and had already reached Prenzlau, which, until recently, had been the seat of the OKH. Those of our comrades that had remained in Neustrelitz while waiting to join us in Berlin would now be engaged in battle. In any case, even if the Wenck Army succeeded in getting through to us, our comrades would not be able to rejoin us.

The day was over, and as the Division feared night infiltrations by the Reds, the battalion was tasked with setting up sentry posts. That night two anti-tank commandos set off for Belle-Alliance-Platz (now Mehringplatz). The first was led by von Wallenrodt, the second by Staff-Sergeant Hennecart. Hennecart was the man who would walk through a hail of shells and bullets with his hands in his pockets and, whenever cautioned, would answer: 'I am already too old to make a corpse.' At 38 years old he was in our eyes an old man, almost ancestral, and the men venerated him. He should have received the epaulets of a second-lieutenant a long time ago, having earned them a hundred times, and should have figured on the 20th April (Hitler's birthday) promotions list. But where was it?

Time passed, but no one came back. The Division was still asking for reinforcements for its sector and, if this went on, all the battalion would soon be engaged. Douroux led me hobbling over the rubble and I do not know what ruined monument to *Stadtmitte* U-Bahn Station, where the general briefed me in detail on the situation. The whole battalion was to be engaged together at Belle-Alliance-Platz to prevent access by the Red tanks and infantry to the Reichs Chancellery via Wilhelmstrasse and Friedrichstrasse. I got up to go. 'Where are you going?' asked the general. 'To get the rest of the battalion going. We should be gone in ten minutes.'

'Don't leave here, you can't even stand! Issue your orders and remain at rest here in the command post.'

'General, it is impossible for me to remain here when all my men are in action!'

'I find it above all impossible that you should not obey my orders,' replied the general. 'Don't insist!'

Time passed slowly in this wretched underground. The Reds did not forget us, for a shell landed on the access stair-case killing or wounding fifteen men. The battle continued to rage all day long and one no longer paid attention to it.

The focal point of the *Nordland*'s defence was Belle-Alliance-Platz, which was defended by a combat team of the *Danmark* under SS-Second-Lieutenant Bachmann, whose sappers attempted to demolish the Hallesche Tor Bridge, but failed to so effectively, leaving sufficient space for tanks to cross. The first Soviet tank did so at 1430 hours, and was promptly destroyed, but others followed.

That evening Combat Team *Dircksen* of the *Danmark* was driven back on Friedrichstrasse to 200m south of *Kochstrasse* U-Bahn station, using the tunnel to withdraw as the Soviets advanced on the surface. Six Soviet tanks reached as far as Wilhlemplatz outside the Reichs Chancellery before they were destroyed.

28 April

The remains of the *Nordland* held positions with the *Norge* Regiment from the Spittelmark on the left flank to Kochstrasse with the *Danmark* Regiment on the right. The armour of SS-Panzer-Regiment 11 and about five *Tiger II*s of SS-Panzer-Battalion 503 were deployed between the Tiergarten, Unter den Linden and Leipziger Strasse.

The *Charlemagne* troops had spent the night either in the

Schauspielhaus cellars or near *Stadtmitte* U-Bahn station, where Eric Lefèvre later described the situation:

> The HQ is now roughly organised. The telephone works. Blankets and sheets separate the different offices and services of the headquarters. One works on tables and chairs taken from here and there, and the boxes. But the lighting is dependent upon candles. There is an intimate, partly unreal atmosphere. Sounds of the battle taking place on the surface are clearly audible. Water from broken pipes oozes down the walls and covers the platform. During the final hours of the night reports from the Combat Team *Dircksen* and from Sector Z Headquarters say that Soviet tanks are still crossing the canal bridge and massing on Belle-Alliance-Platz, indicating powerful new attacks and in depth. General Krukenberg even expects a penetration as far as his own command post. A patrol commanded by SS-Lieutenant von Wallenrodt is despatched towards Wilhelmstrasse to get a precise picture of the situation. Without waiting for his return, the divisional commander sends off two French anti-tank detachments led by SS-Lieutenant Weber and Staff-Sergeant Lucien Hennecart. The first takes men from the Combat School, the second elements of the battalion's liaison team.
>
> At dawn Friedrichstrasse was blocked at the level of Hedemannstrasse by a combat team under SS-Lieutenant Christensen with a nucleus of grenadiers from the *Danmark* Regiment expanded by elements from the Navy, Volkssturm and Labour Service. Obstructed by rubble, pierced by craters and holes in the roof of the U-Bahn tunnel, the street was impassable to tanks, the latter forming a threat only along Wilhelmstrasse upon which it deployed today and on which the French anti-tank detachments concentrated. The leading detachment, commanded by Sergeant Eugène Vaulot, reached as far as the canal west of Belle-Alliance-Platz, but was obliged to pull back under fire from mortars and auto-

matic weapons after having seen the mass of tanks assembled on the square.

Involved here were the 28th and 29th Guards Rifle Corps of General Chuikov's 8th Guards Army at Potsdammerstrasse and along the line of Wilhelmstrasse from Belle-Alliance-Platz respectively, together with General Badanian's 11th Tank Corps and the 50th Guards Tank Regiment, a total of 230 tanks in all. In addition, the 1st Guards Tank Army provided support with the 11th Guards Tank Corps, together with the 11th Independent Guards Tank Regiment equipped with *Josef Stalin 2* tanks.

Eric Lefèvre continued:

A little later, the detachments of SS-Lieutenant Weber and Staff-Sergeant Hennecart took up positions on Wilhelmstrasse adjacent to SS-Lieutenant Christensen's combat team on Hedemannstrasse. Most of the men were concealed behind the ground floor or cellar windows, or inside the entrances to the buildings. Look-outs were deployed behind the heaps of rubble covering the pavements. Suddenly came the throbbing of engines, the characteristic clanking and creaking. A lone tank rolled along Wilhlemstrasse checking the terrain. Sergeant Vaulot raised the grilled sight on his *Panzerfaust* and thumbed forward the safety catch. He calmly aimed the tube on his shoulder with the foresight on the explosive head in line with the lower notch on the grill. He aimed and pressed the trigger. The detonation released a jet of flame to the rear, fatal to anyone in line behind for three metres, and there was a cloud of white smoke. The projectile, stabilised by four flanges, pierced the air at 45 metres per second. Then came the shock of the explosion, the jet of focused gas penetrating the armour with a diameter of ten centimetres, thanks to the hollow charge. A rain of metal fragments projected within the crew space, provoking the ignition of exploding shells and a series of detonations that seemed to shake the heavy machine. Then came the final explosion in a cloud of dust and smoke that dislodged the turret, spreading innumerable bits of debris around. The experienced firer then took care to take cover by crouching against the wall or throwing himself to the ground.

For 'Gégène' – the name given to him by his comrades – it was all in the day's work, but a good job nevertheless. This plumber from Pantin was of a retiring nature, at least with regard to his superiors. In the course of the two years that he had spent in the ranks of the LVF nothing had been said of him, save as an example of discipline and application to the service. As a combatant, he had advanced slowly, no doubt with the encouragement of SS-Lieutenant Weber in the Company of Honour then in the combat school. On the 26th February, during the fighting at Elsenau in Pomerania, he had destroyed a heavy *Josef Stalin* tank, and on the 26th April he had added two more tanks to his score in Neukölln, so this was his fourth.

A change in Soviet tactics then took place that was to be repeated during the fighting. The first phase was the 'cleansing' of the route by 120 mm mortars, the effectiveness of their bombs being at its maximum in a street. Then guns of the tanks, the 85 mm of the *T 34*s, or the 122 mm of the *Josef Stalins*, and the 57 mm anti-tank guns fired their explosive shells directly at the facades of buildings where they had located firers. Under cover of this bombardment, other tanks tried to tow back the wrecks blocking the route. They were to find this more successful under cover of darkness but, for the moment, it was broad daylight. The mounting curls of smoke and the dust suspended in the atmosphere practically blocked out the spring sky. Sticking to the men, it rendered less and less discernible the brown and green flecks on their combat uniforms in which they were nearly all clad. A tenacious smell of burning rubber and decomposing bodies filtered through everywhere. The sounds of battle and the persistent rumblings became less and less perceptible to the ears over accustomed to hearing them.

Fenet resumed: 'Next morning the general seemed better disposed towards me and the report on the battalion's activities clearly pleased him. I took advantage of this to say that I was feeling much better, which was true, although I was still in a bit of a stupor, but fit enough to leave with Finck and his ammunition party.'

Krukenberg continued:

Early on the morning of the 28th April, the Soviets succeeded in crossing the canal in the vicinity of the Hallesches Tor with the aid of numerous auxiliary bridges. From then on the fighting developed building by building and in the heaps of rubble.

Casualties increased on either side. They resulted not only as the result of enemy arms, but also by the collapsing of buildings on which the enemy increasingly concentrated their artillery. Despite this, on that day and the following the grenadiers of the *Nordland* succeeded in holding their set positions against the Soviets with the exception of some local penetrations and breaches. The fighting against their accompanying tanks by self-propelled guns, but above all by the French anti-tank troops, played an important role in the resistance.

Thus Sergeant Eugène Vaulot, having already destroyed two enemy tanks with Panzerfausts within 24 hours in Neukölln, went on to destroy another six Russian tanks in the same manner. On my recommendation, he was awarded the Knight's Cross of the Iron Cross, which I presented to him by candlelight on the morning of the 29th in my command post in the S-Bahn station in the presence of my staff and his French comrades.

In my short address in French, I said that the personal

conduct of this young volunteer was in accordance with what French soldiers were renowned for historically for their bravery on all the world's fields of battle.

In all, the number of enemy tanks definitely knocked out in our sector mounted to 108, of which at least a half was attributable to the French volunteers. This demonstrates well the severity of the fighting and explains why the Soviets were unable to penetrate the front in our sector.

At the divisional command post it was decided to reinforce the forward positions. SS-Major-General Krukenberg decided to keep Captain Fenet with him at this command post.

The majority of the Storm Battalion's men remained in reserve in the cellars of the Schauspielhaus, where some of them amused themselves by donning stage costumes. Some were wounded while collecting rations, for the Soviet artillery and ground-attack aircraft were a constant menace to all movement. Staff-Sergeant Jean Ollivier from the 4th Company had two MG 44s installed in an anti-aircraft role at the entrance to the shelter situated alongside the little public garden next to the French cathedral, and this was how Officer-Cadet Protopopoff, a 'White Russian', succeeded in bringing down one of two aircraft flying over the Gendarmenmarkt.

Captain Fenet resumed:

We all left together after visiting Staff-Sergeant Hennecart, who had been wounded and just been brought in. We found him sitting pensively in one of the carriages serving as a first aid post. He had been hit in the leg and knee during a bombardment and was unable to stand upright.

Finck took me along the tunnels as far as Kochstrasse. Access to the firing position was not at all easy. One had to pass through blocks of buildings and climb down a ladder into a yard to finally arrive at the firing line. SS-Lieutenant Weber, the young combat school commander, a man who needs at least one tank for breakfast every morning, took me into a low room from which one had an excellent view of Wilhelmstrasse . He took me by the arm while putting a finger to his lips and led me to the loophole. 'Look!'

There was a stationary T-34 only three metres away. Its turret bore the mortal wound of a *Panzerfaust*. Short flames were emerging from the transmission and were gently licking the carcass. 'Isn't that a beauty!' said Weber in a low voice. It surely was, and he was the one responsible for this fine bit of work; yet another one. He then gave me a detailed account of the day's work; five or six tanks destroyed with *Panzerfausts*, and numerous infantry attacks repulsed with severe losses for the Reds. However, we were reduced entirely to our own resources; not a tank, gun, mortar, not a single rifle grenade. All we had left were the *Panzerfausts*, assault rifles and several MG-42 machine guns, not much. On the other hand, the Reds in front of us had tanks in plenty. The more we destroyed, the more they replaced them. They still had anti-tank guns, and a pack of 120mm mortars, an infantryman's worst enemy in the open. Their infantry, which had been quite timid until then, now appeared to be quite numerous. But what did that matter, we 'held the Cup' and our men were fighting mad.

At the battalion command post I was received by yells of joy from the runners, who hastened to relate their latest exploits. Really, their tally was quite considerable, and there was no stopping them. Roger and his acolytes located a big building that the Russians had occupied in strength. They had infiltrated the cellars and set light to them, then left to cover the exits and waited patiently. When the fire reached dangerous proportions, the Reds evacuated precipitately without taking any precautions, only to be met by a fusillade from assault rifle grenades that caused carnage. Those who tried to get into the street or courtyards were immediately cut down by the assault rifles, and those who tried to take shelter in the rooms still intact were tackled with hand-grenades.

They were all killed, one after another. When it was over, they had counted about fifty bodies scattered around the building or in the entrance. The operation had taken place at night in the light of the flames. 'It was better than the cinema,' declared Roger.

Krukenberg resumed:

On the morning of the 28th April, the patrols sent towards Belle-Alliance-Platz (especially that led by SS-Lieutenant von Wallenrodt, the battalion adjutant and German liaison officer) failed to return, for the whole battalion was soon engaged on Belle-Alliance-Platz as an anti-tank commando to prevent the Russians access to Wilhelmstrasse and Friedrichstrasse. The Soviets were again checked there with heavy losses.

The main action was near Kochstrasse U-Bahn Station, where five or six tanks were destroyed by the French during the day, who had neither armour, artillery, anti-tank guns, nor mortars, but only several MG-42s, assault rifles and Panzerfausts to oppose the Soviet T-34 tanks, anti-tank guns and 120mm mortars.

A building occupied by the enemy was set on fire by the French, while others covered the windows with assault rifles to prevent the Russians fleeing the flames. Some fifty bodies were counted at this place. The fighting was ferocious, from door to door, window to window.

29 April
Krukenberg continued:

At daybreak a fresh attack by Russian tanks was stalled, but the enemy began a terrible bombardment of all the buildings held by the French. The battle had reached a pitch that was to be maintained to the end. It was hell.

The competitive spirit was such that men took the remaining *Panzerfausts* to claim 'their' tank. Sergeant Roger Albert already had three to his credit.

The enemy fire directed at the French increased, forcing them to withdraw about 50 metres. A new surprise attack was repulsed. Two more tanks were destroyed and one damaged, with the support of our 120mm mortars and nests of resistance.

The battalion sector was almost surrounded once more. A little counterattack by the Main Security Office Germans at the cost of heavy losses permitted the re-alignment of our positions before the next massive tank attack. This failed in its turn, because the first two tanks, having been knocked out, blocked the way for the others. The pounding continued.

Sergeant-Major Rostaing, commanding the 3rd Company (ex 6th Company of Regiment 58), which was uniquely composed of former members of the LVF, received the Iron Cross First Class for his brave conduct and Second-Lieutenant Albert the same for his fourth tank.

The battalion was occupying an advance post of the local defence several hundred metres from the Chancellery. The attacks by Russian tanks soon gave up and Russian infantry infiltrated a little everywhere using flamethrowers or grenades.

The battalion fought on, the lightly wounded returning to their posts as soon as they had been bandaged. Staff-Sergeant Ollivier, commanding the 4th Company, was three times wounded and three times evacuated, but returned three times to his post. Many of the young officer-cadets from Neweklau fell in action: Le Maignan, Billot, and Protopopoff were killed.

The bombardment raged and the city was in flames all night of the 29th–30th April, but all the French SS were resolved to hold out until their ammunition ran out.

Once more we were sustained by high hopes for the arrival

of Wenck's army, but we started becoming sceptical about this subject. We learned nothing about it either from the commander of the city's defence or from the Chancellery.

During a relatively quiet interlude, SS-Lieutenant Weber visited Captain Fenet with Sergeant Vaulot, who had destroyed four tanks in Wilhelmstrasse the previous day, and Sergeant Roger Albert, who had destroyed three. But before the dust had even settled, there was another tank attack with the tanks well spaced out and the leading two were stopped with *Panzerfausts*. The tanks behind withdrew after firing at the buildings. According to Fenet, there was a dramatic situation at his command post:

The floors collapsed and the rooms of our semi-basement were filled with a dust so thick that we had great difficulty in breathing and were unable to see more than 50 centimetres. The ceiling fell in pieces and several of the men were injured by falling masonry. In an angle of the wall where we had made a loophole, there was now a gaping hole in the angle of fire from the tanks.

Moreover, the Soviet infantry were in the process of surrounding the building containing the command post. A little more to the east, in Friedrichstrasse, which was impractical for the tanks, the *Christensen* Combat Team had been in action since dawn. The fighting line was now 150–200m beyond Kochstrasse U-Bahn station and Puttkammerstrasse. Also Soviet infantry were installed in the upper storeys of the neighbouring buildings and firing on anything that moved. But they were not occupying the lower storeys and the French set these buildings on fire with large stocks of paper that they had found in the cellars and could thus use the cover of the fire to effect a withdrawal, despite the protestations of SS-Lieutenant Weber, who wanted to hold on at all costs.

Fenet continued:

The new front line was based on the Puttkamerstrasse cross-roads, 140 to 150 metres further back from the previous one. The internal courtyards here provided relatively safe passage. The new forward command post was installed in a building that was still standing, where it was necessary to block the large entrances, apart from the large gaps made by the bombardment in its façade. The cellars and ground floor, where the men installed themselves, were full of works of art. Two women were still living there and at first refused to leave.

While the new positions were being arranged, the Soviet 120-mm mortars, which had not been heard since the day before, proceeded to reduce to dust those of their infantry that had not broken contact!

No doubt it was at this instant that Officer-Cadet Protopopoff of the 4th Company was killed. He was talking to Sergeant-Major Rostaing in one of the courtyards situated behind the command post building and had been directed towards a porch when a shell exploded in the yard, riddling him with shrapnel.

A catastrophic counterattack was launched by the old officers and NCOs from the Main Security Office, who suffered frightful losses in trying to establish forward look-outs. Then the infantry pressure combined with a fresh tank attack, the third that day. The machines advanced in tight groups of seven or eight, a tactic with the aim of swamping the *Panzerfaust* firers, but the latter were not overawed by this. The two leading tanks were stopped and blocked the route. The five or six others withdrew, then came forward again to tow away the dead ones. Numerous shots with *Panzerfausts* forced them back a second time. The volunteers of the French battalion knew that they had to immediately take cover. However, not all!

When the Soviet tank guns and anti-tank guns concentrated their fire on the basement windows, Sergeant-Major Rostaing remained in his observation post on the second floor of a building offering a good view of Wilhelmstrasse. He had rejoined the battalion that day with the 20 to 25 remaining men of the 3rd Company. Rostaing was in a stairwell with a French grenadier. The two men were flat against the wall on one side and an opening whose glass and frame had long since disappeared. They remembered seeing a vast tank firing, no doubt a *Josef Stalin*. The shell hit the ceiling above two look-outs, covering them with debris and tearing away a main beam that fell on them. Other men witnessed the event. They went up to the storey, called out, but did not see anyone and went down again. The NCO did not recover consciousness for a considerable time later, and got out without difficulty. He staggered to the command post, covered with dust.

It was from Captain Fenet that Sergeant-Major Rostaing learnt that he and Sergeant Albert, who had just destroyed his fourth tank, had been awarded the Iron Cross First Class. The awards were made in the one of the building's interior courtyards. No doubt it was then that SS-Lieutenant von Wallenrodt received his Iron Cross Second Class. Captain Fenet had hardly shaken the hands of the recipients when fresh shells hit the building, raising enormous clouds of dust. 'We stayed there blind, suffocated, without being able to move a step, and it was a while before we regained the use of our senses,' wrote Captain Fenet later.

SS-Lieutenant Christensen had quit his command post on the left at Kochstrasse U-Bahn station to conform with the French, passing round several bottles of wine with which to refresh their throats.

On the other hand, Captain Fenet seemed to have only a hazy picture of the *Müncheberg* Tank Division's sub-sector on the right. Reports coming from there that day indicate otherwise than all communications had been severed with the *Nordland*:

Soviet spearheads have reached the Anhalter Railway Station some 200–300 metres from the French positions. However, a *Tiger II* of SS-Panzer-Regiment *Hermann von Salza*, the '314' of SS-Sergeant Diers – one of the two still at the disposal of the Division – is stationed on Potsdammer Platz and is keeping Saarlandstrasse under fire with its formidable 88mm gun, which has hit several tanks trying to come up the road towards the north-west.

That evening, after several more tank attacks supported by infantry, the problem of effectives became of concern to Captain Fenet, who had seen the number of losses increase, even with the lightly wounded remaining at their posts. He now only had one officer, one officer-cadet and a sergeant-major left, SS-Lieutenant von Wallenrodt, Officer-Cadet Douroux and Sergeant Major Rostaing. Officer-Cadets Protopopoff, Billot, Le Maignan and Karanga had been killed, Officer-Cadet de Lacaze and Staff-Sergeant Ollivier wounded and evacuated. Second-Lieutenant Aimé Berthaud had been evacuated after having been found unconscious under the ruins of a balcony. Officer-Cadets Boulmier and Jacques Frantz had also been evacuated, the latter in a tent-half, after being hit by mortar fire.

Sergeant Eugène Vaulot had also left the front line for the divisional command post after receiving the Knight's Cross that evening in candlelight from SS-Major-General Krukenberg on the station platform, being the first of the French volunteers to receive this decoration. Three other members of the *Charlemagne* were awarded the Knight's Cross that day, making this the record number for any contingent in the battle for the city and demonstrating the importance of their anti-tank role. The destruction of sixty-two tanks, a tenth of the numbers engaged against this sector, was attributed to the *Charlemagne* alone.

During a visit to the Reichs Chancellery first-aid post after having been wounded in the shoulder after destroying his thirteenth Soviet tank, SS-Lieutenant Wilhelm Weber, reported to

SS-Major-General Mohnke, who, greatly impressed, had then recommended Knight's Cross awards for Weber, Captain Fenet and Staff-Sergeant Appolot (six tanks) to General Wilhelm Burgdorf, head of the Army personnel branch.

30 April

Krukenberg continued:

> On the morning of the 30th April, as I learnt later, General Weidling had held a commanders' conference at the Bendlerblock, in which one could speak freely about the situation. But, despite the central importance of his sector, SS-General Mohnke was not invited anymore than myself as commander of the *Nordland* Division, which constituted the main fighting force of the LVIth Panzer Corps, and whose command I had taken over at his request.
>
> The volume of fire on the city centre had increased and our positions subjected to the fire of 'Stalin-Organs'. The battle seemed to be reaching its climax, but the enemy had hardly penetrated our sector and we prepared for more assaults from him. Ammunition and Panzerfausts were deposited along our main line of resistance and on Leipziger Strasse. Unfortunately, four of our tanks, whose guns were still capable of firing, had been immobilised by direct hits.
>
> The usual evening conference at the Sector 'Z' commander was called off without explanation. To our surprise, enemy artillery fire in our sector lessened towards midnight and almost completely ceased.

Captain Fenet resumed his account:

> Now we receive a big reinforcement. A good hundred men from the Main Security Office, armed with rifles and flanked by three or four SS-majors, two SS-Captains and five or six other officers. All are full of good will and courage, but have

long become unaccustomed to handling weapons and lack combat training. Most are between 50 and 60 years old. Nevertheless, their arrival enables a considerable strengthening of the battalion and besides they mix in with plenty of spirit. However, they soon realise that they are in no way prepared for such a pitiless battle. There losses are serious, because the Reds, like ourselves, even more than us, have their elite snipers hidden everywhere and take aim at any silhouette appearing at a window or in a yard.

de Lacaze, who since the beginning of the battle has led his men with astonishing confidence for a debutant, neutralises every attempt by the Red infantry, but he too falls to an enemy sniper and has to be evacuated. Here is Roger again with his usual accomplice, Bicou, at 18 the youngest NCO in the battalion. They are both excited and explain that they have just dislodged several Red snipers from the rooftops.

There are some more there, but we have run out of grenades. While speaking, they are stuffing their pockets with egg grenades, attaching others to the buttons of their jackets, and sticking stick grenades into their belts. They rush off.

Sometime later Bicou returns with his head bowed. 'We got them, captain, but Roger was wounded.'

Roger comes in paler than usual, a trickle of blood running from his right eye. At the last moment a piece of grenade caught him above the eyelid. We sit him down in the only armchair in the building, where he soon dozes off. A little later Bicou takes him to the medical aid post with a group of wounded, then comes back alone.

'Poor Roger, the fighting is over for him. The doctor says that the eye is lost and he still does not know whether he can save the other one.'

Bicou himself is lucky. During the day he had taken shelter behind a pile of debris that was hit by an anti-tank shell. He didn't even get a scratch, but was knocked unconscious. An hour later he was on his feet again. Now he takes over the section with a sombre air, vowing that Roger's eye will cost dear.

It is quite calm as night draws to an end. There is nothing in the street but the T–34 burning alongside us, long flames dancing around the steel carcass, projecting their violent light against the dark night which the rose-coloured halo of fires above the roofs is unable to disperse. One hears the crackling of the flames mixing with the distant, confused sounds of fighting in the capital. But sometimes we are startled by heartbreaking cries, cries that are no longer human, the voices of women not far from us howling in their distress, despair and anguish as the men from the steppes assert their bestiality.

With daybreak the Red tanks set off again and we are alerted by the sound of their engines starting up. Several well directed *Panzerfausts* and the first wave is easily stopped, because the tanks are following each other well spaced out, which gives us plenty of time to see them coming and to give each one the greeting it deserves.

Of course, having checked this first attempt, we are subjected to the usual bombardment. The tanks and anti-tank guns fire full out at the buildings where they detect our presence. The walls tremble dangerously, plaster falls on our heads, and sometimes a well aimed shot into a window opening or loophole showers us with earth and stones and plunges us into a spell of powdery obscurity. Already yesterday and nightfall were hard enough, but now the battle is about to reach a climax and maintain it to the end. Up to this point we have been living in an infernal din, pounded ceaselessly by mortars, anti-tank guns and tanks, harassed by the infantry, repelling several tank attacks an hour. Weber, whose tally is already quite considerable, brings a young NCO from his combat school, Sergeant Eugène Vaulot, a tall, blond chap who has already bagged four tanks since yesterday, another sergeant, Roger Albert, who has his third and is claiming a fourth. As there are not enough Panzerfausts for everyone, they all want the chance to bag at least one tank.

The more our resistance hardens, the more the enemy fires at us. In the command post building, which has become the main point of resistance, we expect the walls to collapse over our heads at any moment. The façade is already completely cracked and one can feel the building sway with every blow. Sooner or later we will have to evacuate or be wiped out or buried, but I delay the departure as long as possible, for the configuration of the area is such that if we evacuate this building, our whole front will have to pull back at least 50 metres if we are want to find another suitable location, and 50 metres now is not that easy. We are only several hundred metres from the Reichs Chancellery.

No doubt believing us *hors de combat*, the Reds launch another tank attack, but this time without an artillery preparation, but we are not dead yet. The result is two tanks destroyed and a third damaged. The attacking wave turns round. Now they are going to make us pay for this disappointment. Once the tanks are out of range of our *Panzerfausts*, they aim their guns at us again and every barrel they have fires at us. The upper storeys collapse, the rooms of our semi-basement are filled with such thick dust that we can hardly breathe and we can only see 50 centimetres in front of us. The ceiling falls in pieces and several men are injured by falling masonry. The loophole that we had made in the angle of the wall has become a gaping hole right in line with the tanks' line of fire. The next bombardment will bring a general collapse. Moreover, the Russians are working dangerously on our left wing and are making their way across the ruins to encircle our whole block of buildings, and all our exits are now under fire. Nevertheless, we have to leave; in ten minutes it will be too late. Our troops are engaged in neutralising the Red snipers stationed in a big building opposite from the neighbouring houses. Their building has vast cellars, which the Ivans have neglected to occupy that are full of enormous quantities of paper. We set them on fire and, while Ivan plays fireman, we get out. Saluted on our way by several burst of fire and some grenades, we manage to get through without losses and cross the field of ruins that separates us from our new positions without difficulty. Only one building in three is still standing in this area.

According to Krukenberg, this move took place at 1800 hours.

The new front will be easier to defend, for a system of interior courtyards provides excellent communications protected from the enemy, a small compensation for the 50 metres we have just lost. There is only one dangerous corner, alongside Friedrichstrasse, where a ruined building, very difficult to keep an eye on, offers our opponents magnificent possibilities for infiltration.

We quickly set up our sentries, for the Reds are not going to waste any time. Our old east front enemies, the 120mm mortars, take us on and keep lashing us right until the very end, harassing us with the diabolical precision to which they are accustomed. The infantry too engage strongly. We have to mount a little attack in order to set up new forward positions to obtain a little peace, relatively speaking. This is done by the men from the Main Security Office, who carry out the operation with remarkable spirit. Unfortunately, for lack of support from heavy weapons, our losses are very heavy.

While the infantry are fighting it out furiously, another tank attack begins. This time the Reds have taken into account the errors they have been making until now. Instead of arriving one by one to serve as ideal targets for our *Panzerfausts*, seven or eight set off together and remain bunched together, only a few metres apart from each other. They want to make us concentrate to maintain the effectiveness of our fire. Fortunately, our men are up to this change of tactics. The two leading tanks block the middle of the street, barring the way for the others, who are obliged to turn around. Shortly afterwards there is another alarm, this time the Reds are trying to tow away their wrecks to clear the street for their next attack, so again there a fine scrap.

We have hardly time to draw breath before the next shelling begins. Sergeant-Major Rostaing, commanding No. 3 Company, is buried under the debris of his observation post on the second floor. They call him and someone climbs up to the second floor with difficulty, but nothing moves, where is he under all this debris? An hour later he reappears, somewhat haggard, saying that he had been knocked unconscious by the fall of the ceiling, and had only just regained consciousness.

I award him the Iron Cross First Class in a little courtyard nearby, and also Roger Albert, who has just bagged his fourth tank. While we are shaking hands, another tornado falls on us, raising clouds of dust so thick that we remain blinded, suffocated, unable to move a foot, no longer knowing where we are, and it takes a moment or two before we regain the use of our senses.

We begin to get bad headaches. Outrageously smothered with dust, our eyes shining, deep in their sockets, our cheeks lined, we hardly look human. Water is scarce and we often don't even have enough to drink. Occasionally a few rations arrive from Division. One eats what one can find, when one can find it, otherwise, in the feverish state we are in, it is not a problem that concerns us much. After the days we have just been through, we are now only acting on our reflexes, and everything we do seems as natural as everyday life. We seem to have been living this infernal life for ever, the problem of the future does not even arise, and we see ahead of us more days like this, knocking out tanks, firing at the Reds, throwing grenades, alarms, bombardments, fires, ruins, holding on, not allowing the enemy to pass. All our strength, all our energy is only for this, it is simultaneously our reason for living and for dying.

I get visitors from time to time, particularly from an officer of the *Nordland* commanding a neighbouring company. He comes, he says, to refresh himself with us, although he does not seem to need it. He does not hesitate to express his admiration for his French comrades. Every time he comes he repeats: 'While you are there, we are content that all is well and certain that the sector will hold.' He only knows how to show his sympathy, and thanks to him, we can pass around several bottles of wine, from which everyone drinks a symbolic mouthful with pleasure.

In one place or another, our frontline positions are shrivelling up, and we are now in front of the lines, an advance defence post in front of the Reichs Chancellery. Also, more and more the Reds hound us. We no longer keep count of the tank attacks, the infantry are more and more aggressive, and abandoning frontal assaults, now attempt to penetrate a little everywhere to dislodge us with grenades or flame-throwers. If the Red's losses are high, our effectives are also diminishing, even though only the severely wounded are evacuated; the others make do with a summary bandaging and carry on fighting, or take a few hours' rest in the first aid post before returning to their positions. Staff-Sergeant Ollivier, commanding No. 4 Company, beats all records in this field. Hit three times, three times evacuated, he has calmly returned to his post three times. Our young officers, second-lieutenants and officer-cadets, have already paid a high price: Labourdette, Le Maignan, Billot, Protopopoff, killed, de Lacaze, Bert, François, Ulmier, seriously wounded. Weber, who since the beginning has shown an extraordinary ardour, and has put all his energy into it, has been evacuated in his turn with a serious injury. In all the unit only Douroux and von Wallenrodt remain uninjured among the officers. Douroux is very proud of the fact that an officer of the *Nordland* removed his own Iron Cross to award him with it after an engagement in which he had performed marvellously. As for von Wallenrodt, he remains very calm and very much at ease in all this din, a former war correspondent, he is at once both spectator and actor, acquitting himself remarkably in his new role as adjutant. He also receives a well earned Iron Cross.

The command post is in a large library that has some magnificent works of art. One of us has pulled out an album of coloured pictures of Spain, which becomes a distraction for men taking a break. We flip through it in search of sunny country scenery as an antidote to our vision of hell. Passing the rows of bookshelves, I am angered by the thought that they will become victims to the flames, or worse, will be torn up and trampled underfoot by bands of drunken Mongols.

We are living in scenes from another world: the days are the colour of the dust that overcomes and devours us. We no longer see the blue sky, being absorbed in a gritty fog that only dissipates at rare moments until a new torrent of missiles plunge us back into yellowish opaqueness. Buildings are burning everywhere, ruins collapse with a great noise, thickening the atmosphere with soot, dust and smoke, which we breathe with difficulty. The silence that follows a bombardment is only the prelude to a roaring of engines, the clanking of tracks, announcing another wave of tanks. Crouched in the doorways or behind windows with *Panzerfausts* in our hands, we await our turn to release the storm. A long tongue of flame behind the firer, a violent explosion, shortly followed by another marking the arrival of a mortal blow, almost always firing at point blank range, which is more certain. The explosions follow each other within several seconds: one, two, sometimes three tanks are immobilised in the middle of the street. The others retire and several minutes later they return to tow back the dead carcasses under cover of clouds of dust raised by the bombardment that always follows an aborted attack.

The battle continues to rage throughout the night. How can one describe the night? Darkness, chased away by this enormous brazier that the city has become, has vanished and only the colour of the light varies by the hour. The burning buildings and tanks are our torches, and Berlin is illuminated by the fire devouring it. A sinister clarity hangs over the city, now suffused with a reddish glow on which the flames rising around us shed their violent light. Beneath this tragic display the ruins cutting the incandescent sky take on unreal, incredible shapes,

The rumbling upheaval of the battle has now submerged all the city, which fiercely struggles and fights on not to let itself be engulfed by defeat, prolonging its hopeless agony to the extreme limit. In this duel to death, as the hours pass and the enemy accumulates against us more tanks, more men, more shells, our determination only grows, our resolution hardens more. Hold on, the words always returns to our lips, invades our spirit as an obsession. Hold on, as if tomorrow will be like today, like yesterday. Until when? The question no longer arises: as long as we have bullets, grenades, *Panzerfausts*. The Red infantry continue to bite the dust, the tanks, despite their furious assaults, are checked in front of or inside our lines, where they burn in agony. We can see the flames emerging between the tracks, then climbing progressively up to the turret, while the ammunition explodes in an uninterrupted series of detonations that shake the steel carcass belted with fire until a formidable explosion shakes the whole area, sending enormous chunks of steel flying until nothing remains of the tank but a mass of twisted, blackened scrap.

On the evening of the 30th April a Russian is brought to the command post who had allowed himself to be captured without difficulty. He is a Ukrainian NCO, a big, well fed lad. He brings with him several loaves of bread, which the men share between them with pleasure, for they haven't seen anything like that for several days. In exchange the prisoner is given cigarettes, which seems to please him. Very talkative, he explains to the interpreter that he is Ukrainian and not Russian. Compulsorily mobilised, and a ferocious adversary of bolshevism, so much so that we could not have a better friend than himself in the Red Army. Of course we are under no illusions about the sincerity of his good will, but we pretend to listen with interest. Confident, he chats with the interpreter, replying at length to the questions negligently put to him during the course of the conversation. A communiqué has been distributed in the Red lines today announcing imminent victory; there is only one square kilometre left in Berlin to be taken, and this last bastion must be taken by tomorrow in honour of the 1st May. A burst of laughter greets the translation of these last words: 'We will still be here tomorrow, old chap, and your pals will get the same as usual if they try and pass!'

He recognises that we are giving them a hard time and that morale in the area leaves much to be desired, but we don't believe our ears when he adds that the tank crews will only board at pistol point. The interpreter asks good humouredly if he is kidding us. 'Niet! Those getting into the leading tanks know that they will not be coming back!'

SS-Major-General Krukenberg resumed his account:

During the night and morning of the 1st May the battle continued with extreme violence. The Russians were glued to the ground with the fire from our assault rifles. That afternoon the enemy resorted to using flamethrowers to reduce isolated points of resistance, an effective tactic, for there was no water to extinguish the flames.

Tuesday, the 1st May, at about 0700 hours in the morning, I was summoned by telephone by SS-General Mohnke, who told me that during the night General Krebs (a former military attaché in Moscow), Colonel von Dufing and Lieutenant Colonel Seifert had crossed the lines in the latter's sector to conduct negotiations with the Soviets. He could not give me the exact details about this mission, but he gave the impression that one could no longer count upon being relieved by Wenck's army, which had been forced to withdraw by superior enemy forces.

Contrary to expectations, General Krebs and his companions, for whom those opposite had guaranteed free access, had still not returned or reported their news, despite an existing radio link. He suggested a possibility of betrayal and said that now the Soviets knew the weakness of our defences we could now expect a sudden attack.

We had been able to establish that the Potsdammer Platz S- and U-Bahn stations were not barricaded, thus offering an opportunity for an enemy shock troop to approach the Chancellery via Voss-Strasse. I should do the necessary in this respect, but before all else, go to the Air Ministry and take charge of the Seifert sub-sector from its commander. It seemed to him that there were things going on there that I should suppress by all means.

I crossed Wilhelmplatz under enemy fire accompanied by a Franco-German escort and advanced along Wilhelmstrasse as far as the Air Ministry, on which there were no security guards, although the Russian mortars and anti-tank guns were only several hundred yards away.

There was an old Luftwaffe general asleep in the cellars of the Air Ministry with a hundred airmen. Then I came across a young army captain, who was the staff watch keeper for the sub-sector, who told me that Lieutenant Colonel Seifert, having told him he had no need of anyone, had shut himself in his office with his liaison officer to apparently destroy documents. I immediately went with him to the sector command post in which he was the only member of Lieutenant Colonel Seifert's staff. We entered into a lively discussion, during which, having explained my mission, he refused to tell me what had happened the day before, nor where his commander was, when the latter entered the room escorted by two NCOs from my escort, having found him in another part of the building.

Soon afterwards a message arrived from Mohnke's command post explaining what had happened was due to a misunderstanding and that the order given that morning was now nul and void.

I returned to my sector at about 1000 hours, not before begging Lieutenant Colonel Seifert to finally return the men of the *Nordland* and the Frenchmen that were still in his sector.

Towards noon I received an order to immediately place the last 'Tiger' tank of our tank battalion at SS-General Mohnke's disposition. No indication of what was happening at higher level filtered through to us.

At 1900 hours I was summoned by SS-General Mohnke and took my operations officer (Ia) and adjutant with me. SS-Major-General Ziegler approached me in the antechamber to the command post, saying: 'It has just been announced that Hitler committed suicide yesterday afternoon. Apparently he married Fegelein's sister-in-law. The latter tried to flee from the Chancellery in civilian clothes and has been shot. Goebbels and his family are also dead!'

Then SS-General Ziegler added that for several days now no one had expected Wenck's army to succeed, and that the negotiations with the west, entered into with too great an optimism, had failed. We had been deceived from above on all these points for several days now. All the sacrifices made by the troops had been in vain. We had been abused in the worst possible way. How was I going to tell those under my command when I could reproach myself most for my good faith?

SS-General Mohnke appeared after a long wait accompanied by Reich Youth Leader Axmann and in short sentences told me what I already knew from SS-General Ziegler. Then he recalled the nocturnal attempt by General Krebs to obtain an immediate stop to the fighting in Berlin to prevent any further shedding of blood. General Chuikov facing us refused and demanded an unconditional surrender.

This was unacceptable. Thus, basing himself on a very old order, SS-General Mohnke asked me if I, being the most senior officer in my rank, would continue to assure the defence of the city, in which case all troops still available would be placed under my command. I rejected this stupid idea.

Then, he said, there is nothing else to do than follow the order already given by General Weidling for the remainder of the Berlin garrison to attempt to pierce the Soviet encirclement in small groups. In answer to my question, he said that the rest was up to every one of us; the general direction was Neuruppin and then on in a north-westerly direction.

Everything was now on the move. It was impossible to obtain information about the situation in other parts of the city. Each of the groups assembling with a view to breaking out had to make its own necessary reconnaissance.

Finally, in order to avoid chaos, the news of the death of Hitler and the other events we had been told about were not to be divulged until 2100 hours that evening. According to General Weidling's orders issued to all sectors, the defence would cease everywhere at 2300 hours.

All the rest, including the choice of routes, was left to the individual sectors. No rear guard was anticipated. SS-General Ziegler said that he would rejoin the *Nordland* for the breakout. In leaving the Chancellery, I saw no disorder in the rooms or corridors.

The commanders had carte blanche for the careful withdrawal of their troops from 2300 hours onwards, the little posts remaining behind until midnight would mask the total evacuation of our positions from the enemy. At midnight, Regiments *Norge* and *Danmark* left Leipziger Strasse, heading north via Charlottenstrasse and Friedrichstrasse. The U-Bahn tunnel could only be used under the most disciplined conditions and with intervals between groups. It was nevertheless necessary to leave it at Friedrichstrasse S-Bahn Station, for the tunnel was blocked by a solid grille preventing passage under the Spree.

In fact this 'grille' was a waterproof steel bulkhead, normally closed at night for security reasons, and had a guard of two transport-authority watchmen, who refused to open it as to do so would be against regulations!

We took a pause to regroup and decide north of the Spree near the Grand Opera. I myself was in Albrechtstrasse attempting to explore the possibilities with some officers who knew the area well.

Having abandoned my command post a little after midnight and taken the convenient route with my staff and the accompanying French detachment, I sent my liaison officer, SS-Second Lieutenant Patzak to the Air Ministry to collect the men of the *Nordland* and the French still in that sector. According to a report by Captain Fenet, the latter were engaged in the vicinity of Prinz-Albrecht-Strasse. It is not known whether this officer reached there or whether he was killed on the way. Captain Fenet never received my orders.

1 May
Captain Fenet continued his account:

That Ukrainian hadn't lied. All night and all morning of the 1st May the storm of the Red assaults beats against us with desperate violence, but we are determined to respond with defiance. The Red infantry has been reinforced and launches waves of attack simultaneously with the setting off of the tanks. We let the T-34s approach to fire at point blank range, while pinning down the infantry with our assault rifles. The latter try to advance again, but they don't get far and soon they don't get up again.

The Russian concentrate their tanks barely 300 metres away, and the infantry move round behind that steel barrier. We know the buildings they are using, from where the deluge of fire fails to crush us, and of which we easily have the advantage. We have to wait until they are quite close at the end of a rifle or *Panzerfaust*, so close that several missed shots could open up the way and cause the front to collapse. The fate of the battle depends on the outcome of every attack. The Reichs Chancellery is being fiercely defended. One moment of weakness, one inattention on our part, and we would have the catastrophe that threatens, always more precisely to the extent that it consumes our strength and our effectives go on in this battle of hell.

During a particularly violent attack, a T-34 succeeds in passing and is only knocked out 30 metres behind our first position. For several moments a terrible anxiety seizes us, as if an abyss has opened beneath our feet. But no, it cannot be said that a Red tank has succeeded in penetrating our lines with impunity. There is a second explosion and the intruder is immobilised.

The situation worsens during the afternoon. Our building, practically intact when we occupied it, has now fallen into ruins, and if the ground floor is still holding, long strips of parquet are hanging down to the street, a perfect target for the Red flame-throwers, who, taking advantage of the scarcity of out troops, infiltrate through the ruins. We try to get these awkward bits of wood to fall into the street, but without tools in the middle of tottering walls and under enemy fire, our men can only establish the uselessness of their efforts. After several fruitless attempts, the Reds succeed in setting fire to this hanging pyre. We haven't got a drop of water. Georges, the signaller, a placid, smiling, young Norman with plump cheeks, does his best in his quality as a former Parisian fireman, but soon he has to report that we must abandon all hope. If all goes well, we should be able to remain another hour, not more!

The Main Security Office had been decided upon as our next centre of resistance, several dozen metres away. While waiting, we continue the battle with the flames over our heads, while Georges and several others try desperately to slow down the fire's advance at the risk of being burnt alive. After alternatives of hope and anxiety, Georges, black as a charcoal burner, returns to report that there is not much time left; the ground floor will be engulfed in its turn and the hundreds of books ranged along the shelves will provide the flames magnificent nourishment. The ground floor fills with smoke and flames come from the ceiling. It is now impossible to reach Wilhemstrasse. Regretfully, we must leave. It is now 1800 hours.

The Main Security Office is in ruins, but its cellars opening unto the street still provide useful shelter. Our sentries take up their positions without any reaction from the Reds. In fact our move was conducted as discreetly as possible. Soon a violent infantry fight starts up on our right, a furious fusillade opening up and nourished by both sides. The Reds advance and are repulsed, advance again and are again repulsed. Finally they manage to gain a little ground in the neighbouring sector, but our front remains unaltered.

In a cellar serving as a shelter and rest place, and by the light of a candle, I award Iron Crosses to a certain number of our comrades. To be decorated at the front in the course of an impressive parade is everyone's dream, but tonight the pathos of this so simple ceremony with a few gathered round in this dark and narrow cellar during the last hours of a super-human battle is worth all the parades in the world. By the trembling light of this symbolic candle, whose flame cele-brates the victory of light over the shadows and hope over death, the blackened, dull, emaciated faces, creased with fatigue and hunger, the faces tense or shining, with feverish, ardent eyes, take on an extraordinary aspect. 'In the name of the Führer . . .'

The last night is relatively calm. A neighbouring company leaves on a mission on behalf of the Reichs Chancellery and we take over their sector. The *Nordland*'s command post has moved out of Stadtmitte U-Bahn Station and is now in the Reichs Chancellery itself. Dufour, sent there, reports that all is well. This evening they are celebrating the award of the Knight's Cross to Vaulot, who destroyed his seventh tank today, and our few comrades there – the commander kept back several at his disposal – are singing and drinking with their German comrades of the *Leibstandarte Adolf Hitler*. We haven't been forgotten, and Dufour and his group have brought us some chocolate and several bottles. The 1st May, a fateful day, has passed much more successfully than the Ukrainian predicted the other evening.

2 May
Captain Fenet concluded his account:

Towards daybreak, our sentries report that we are again alone ahead of the lines. I check, it is true; there is no one to left or right of us. A little later a patrol reports that the front line is now back to the Air Ministry. We withdraw there during the course of the morning and make contact with the Luftwaffe troops occupying the building. We take up our new positions without any loss of time, but we have hardly done so when we see vehicles bearing white flags coming from the enemy lines. In them are German officers and Russians. There is talk of capitulation. Soon unarmed Russian soldiers come forward offering cigarettes, and some of the Luftwaffe soldiers start fraternising. Other Red soldiers arrive in detachments, but they come from within our lines.

The Luftwaffe commander tells me of his intention of surrendering when the Reds invite him to. 'Its over,' he adds, 'the capitulation has been signed.' But he is unable to provide me with any details. No, we cannot believe that it is all over, that's impossible! In any case, we cannot remain here to be taken stupidly! What's happening at the Reichs Chancellery? There at least we should learn something, and if there is a last square to be formed, we will be the ones to form it!

We quickly leave the ministry without responding to the Reds, men and women, that cordially invite us to hand over our arms. Avoiding the streets, we filter through the ruins as far as the U-Bahn and climb down through a ventilation shaft. There is no living soul at Stadtmitte Station, only two or three empty bags. We then come to the Kaiserhof Station, just behind the Reichs Chancellery. A ladder goes up to a ventilation grid at street level. I am the first to go up and look, my ears attuned to sounds of combat, but there is only the noise of klaxons and moving trucks. More bars, but at last I can see, with my hands clasping the ladder, my eyes take in the spectacle that my body rejects. As far as I can see are Russians, vehicle with the red star going in all directions, not a single shot, the Reichs Chancellery walls are dumb, there is no one around, it is all over!

I go back down again without saying a word. The men gather round me with wide eyes. 'Nobody! The Russians are there, everywhere. The Führer is certainly dead.' They lower their heads in silence.

'Now, we have to get out of here. In my opinion the only solution is to try to get through to the west. We will use the U-Bahn tunnels as long as possible. Let's go! We will get out of this situation this time too! Does everyone agree?'

With our ears pricked we continue on our way. The ceiling has collapsed in several places, in other places rubble blocks the way and we clear a path through with our hands and bayonets. But at Potsdammer Platz a cruel discovery awaits us; from here on the U-Bahn lines are in the open.

It would be best to remain hidden underground and wait for nightfall. One of the tunnels opens under a railway bridge and is blocked with debris, offering a wonderful hiding place. We quickly split up into small groups and vanish one after another. However, some Volkssturm arrive at the same time with the same intention as ourselves. These poor old chaps are slow and noisy, attracting the attention of a Red patrol that enters several seconds later. 'Don't shoot! Don't shoot!' the first Volkssturm calls out in an anxious voice as they grab hold of him. The Reds carefully search the whole area and flush out our group one after another. We hold our breath as the Russians go past. Several times they stop right in front of us. Our hearts beat to breaking point. Pressed one against the other, we wait and cling stubbornly to our last hopes.

The end comes suddenly. Our protecting wall collapses under angry booting, the Russians surround us and comb through our pockets. The first things they take are our watches, and then our weapons. We are dragged outside, where we see drunken groups of the victors staggering around. A swaying Russian approaches us with angrily blinking eyes and threatening mouth. He grabs Roger Albert marching next to me and pushes him against a wall. A guard intervenes and pulls his prisoner back into the column. 'I thought I had had it!' whispers Roger Albert to me. At this moment the drunken Russian returns, seizing his victim again: 'SS! SS!' he cries, pulling out his pistol. A shot rings out and Roger Albert falls at my feet without a sound. Seeing that we are about to stop, our guards push us on shouting, and we continue on our way.

We come to the Reichs Chancellery, which is being ransacked, while hundreds and hundreds of tanks parade through the Tiergarten towards the Brandenburg Gate, which still raises its mutilated profile like a last hope, a last act of defiance.

Rostaing and sixteen other French survivors were sleeping exhausted in the ruins of Potsdammer railway station at around midnight when they were awakened by a call to surrender or the station would be blown up.

General Krukenberg concluded his account:

Having crossed the Spree, I sent the two officers that lived locally off on reconnaissance, but neither of them returned, so towards 0300 hours on the morning of the 2nd May I made a reconnaissance myself accompanied by my French detachment. An attempt to go through the Charité Hospital failed because Professor Sauerbruch (the hospital director), in agreement with the Russian command, had declared it a neutral zone, so I tried to go via Chausseestrasse. I encountered elements of the *Nordland* with SS-General Ziegler, who had joined us with his companions. There were four or five holders of the Knight's Cross of the Iron Cross in our group, including the Frenchman Vaulot.

Meanwhile day was dawning and the Soviets, seeing our column, brought it under violent fire. We turned around with the hope of leaving via Gesundbrunnen towards Pankow and from there on to Wittenau.

Following Brunnenstrasse we were suddenly hit by well directed mortar fire at the level of Lortzingstrasse, apparently coming from the railway ring. We sought shelter in the court-yard of a building on the corner, where SS-General Ziegler was mortally wounded near me by explosions that wounded other members of our group. Soviet infantrymen that had infiltrated the quarter took us under fire in turn, obliging us to turn back towards the city.

At the level of Ziegelstrasse we saw the 'Tiger' tank I had placed at the disposal of the Chancellery the day before, burnt out and abandoned, with no trace of its crew. All the area, including the Weidendammer Bridge, was still clear of the enemy at 0900 hours that morning.

By 1500 hours all resistance had definitely ceased in Berlin. That evening the German armies in Italy and Austria also capitulated.

Having succeeded in hiding myself away with some friends in Dahlem for several days, I eventually surrendered to the Soviet authorities in Berlin-Steglitz.

The known success of the *Charlemagne* contingent in the battle for Berlin is summarised in the following table:

Name	Formerly	Tanks	Decoration	Fate
SS-Lt Wilhelm Weber	SS	8	Knight's Cross	
Sgt Eugène Vaulot	Navy	8	Knight's Cross	Killed
Ssgt François Appolot	Navy	6	Knight's Cross	
Sgt Jules Bocau	SS	4	Iron Cross I	
Gren Claude		4	Iron Cross I	Wounded
Sgt François de Lannurien	SS	3	Iron Cross I	
Sgt Albert	SS	4	Iron Cross I	Killed
Gren Audry	LVF	2		Killed
Gnr Blaise		1		Killed
Gren Aubin		1		

Chapter Nine

Finale

The events in Berlin did not signal the end of the *Charlemagne* as such. There was still the group left behind at Carpin and about another 1,200 men at Wildflecken

The three trucks carrying ninety men of the Storm Battalion that had found their route to Berlin cut returned to Carpin, and the elements of the second echelon were reorganised. The remnants of the Division, amounting to 700 men, of which 400 were now non-combatants, prepared for the final offensive across the Lower Oder as part of the 9th Panzer Army.

At 0700 hours on 20 April, following a short but intensive artillery preparation, the Soviets crossed the Oder south of Stettin. Counterattacks with the feeble forces available on the 21st failed and the Soviets were soon attacking the second line of defence. On 25 and 26 April, while the remains of the Division were still reorganising, the Soviet masses crossed the river at different points and broke out of the Schwedt bridgehead. Stettin was surrounded on the 25th and the Oder front collapsed. The line Prenzlau–Pasewalk held out until the evening of the 26th, but was breached at Prenzlau the next day.

At 1000 hours on 27 April a Soviet spearhead of seventy tanks was reported only 15km from Carpin. It was the end. The Soviets pressed on fiercely, overwhelming all opposition, and the remains of the *Wallonien*, *Langemarck* (Flemish) and Latvian SS Divisions, together with the 1st Naval Division, withdrew to the line Neustrelitz–Neubrandenburg.

The remains of the *Charlemagne* were organised roughly as follows:

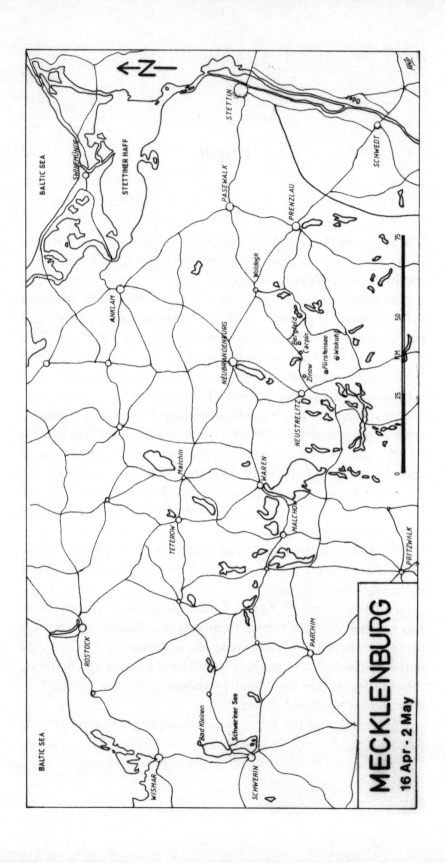

MECKLENBURG
16 Apr - 2 May

Commander:	SS-Colonel Zimmermann (but hospitalised in Neustrelitz)
Deputy Commander:	Major Boudet-Gheusi (1) SS-Captain Hochhauser
Liaison Officer and Ic:	SS-Second-Lieutenant Bender
Reserves:	Lieutenant Bénétoux (IIa/b) Lieutenant Audibert Second-Lieutenant Radici

Battalion 58

Commander:	SS-Captain Kroepsch
5th Company:	Officer-Cadet Aumon
7th Company:	Lieutenant Fatin
8th Company:	Second-Lieutenant Jacques Sarrailhé

Construction Battalion

Commander:	Captain Roy

Medical & Veterinary Services

IVb:	Lieutenant Dr Métais
IVd:	Second-Lieutenant Verney

Motor Transport

IVa:	SS-Captain Hagen
IVb:	SS-Lieutenant Meier

The *Charlemage* no longer came under the 9th Panzer Army's Rear Services and was tasked with defending the anti-tank barrier at Carpin with one company and the Fürstensee barriers on the Berlin–Neustrelitz road with the other two companies.

At 1800 hours on 27 April, Major Boudet-Gheusi moved the divisional headquarters behind the barriers to Zinow. Next morning an armoured division of the Wehrmacht made an unsuccessful counterattack towards Woldeck, and that evening the Russians occupied Bergfeld at 1800 hours.

Major Boudet-Gheusi withdrew his headquarters to Neustrelitz and sent the company that had been guarding the Carpin anti-tank barrier, but meanwhile relieved by the Wehrmacht, to join the two other companies at the Drewin and Fürstensee anti-tank barriers.

The situation was critical, for the enemy, attacking from the southeast, had almost surrounded Neustrelitz from the north and Neubrandenburg had already fallen. With foresight, the Construction Battalion had been sent two days previously to the Malchin area and beat a retreat towards Teterow-Gustrow, while the motor transport withdrew rapidly towards Waren and Malchow.

Since the previous day, the Army Group had been under the command of Luftwaffe-Colonel-General Kurt Student, with General Kurt von Tippelskirch reluctantly standing in temporarily for him.

All the Army Group was in full retreat and for three days of forced marching, the isolated elements of the *Charlemage*, harassed by Allied aircraft, hampered by columns of refugees and mixed up in a flood of diverse elements of the 3rd Panzer, 12th and 21st Armies, made their way across Mecklenburg at increasing speed to escape the constant threat of encirclement by the Russians.

On the evening of 1 May, the exhausted units reached the line Wismar–Schwerin, but the rapid advance of the 2nd British Army's VIIIth Corps had already cut off the route to Denmark, the only way out. The Mecklenburg pocket was sealed with the remains of the Division inside.

The capture of the Baltic port of Wismar by the British 6th Airborne Division and Soviet troops put paid to Major Cance's plans for saving the remains of the *Charlemagne*. Cance, who had been wounded in the foot in the Carpathians in 1944 and subsequently served as director of the SS Franco-Wallonian Officers' School at Kienschlag (Neweklau) and then at SS Main Office in Berlin, had made plans for the evacuation of the retreating French troops to Sweden by sea, for which he had chartered some ships in Wismar harbour. When the French failed to arrive in time, some Wehrmacht elements appropriated the chartered vessels.

At 0900 hours on 2 May, Major Boudet-Gheusi assembled the fifty men accompanying him in a village near Bad Kleinen and permitted them to either disguise themselves as civilian labourers or to surrender themselves to the British with him. The Germans, with SS-Second-Lieutenant Bender in charge, were ordered to try and rejoin a German unit that was still fighting.

At 1500 hours, Major Boudet-Gheusi, Lieutenants Bénétoux and Métais, Second-Lieutenant Radici, one NCO and three men surrendered to an English unit occupying the railway station at Bublitz. When Major Boudet-Gheusi presented himself to an English officer as 'commander of the Legion of French Volunteers against Bolshevism' he was immediately made to climb on a tank with Second-Lieutenant Radici to be taken to Wismar for handing over to the Russians, but the two officers managed to escape when night fell and rejoined the other prisoners of war unnoticed.

SS-Captain Kroepsch's 58th Battalion, which had lost its 6th Company to the Berlin contingent, conducted a delaying action for two days with its remaining three companies deployed as follows:

5th Company:	Holding the anti-tank barrier south of the village of Fürstensee on the Berlin road, thus facing south with the support of one of our last 150mm heavy infantry guns
7th Company:	Deployed in advance positions the first day, it was deployed on the left of the 5th Company on the second day
8th Company:	Deployed facing east astride the road from Fürstensee to Wokuhl. Destroyed two or three tanks during the final fighting.

A marsh and then a line of small lakes extended east–west to the west of the Neustrelitz–Fürstensee–Berlin road in line with the barriers manned by the battalion. The Berlin–Neustrelitz railway passed between the marsh and the lakes and was mined with big spherical naval mines. Further west was the line of retreat assigned to the battalion. Behind these positions, but in front of Fürstensee and alongside the road, was a very important anti-aircraft ammunition depot.

On 28 April the first Soviet elements advanced to contact. Towards 2100 hours the ammunition depot suddenly blew up without warning, wiping out a column of 2–3,000 inmates of Oranienburg Concentration Camp with their guards.

The Russians attacked on the 29th, and eventually the remains of the battalion withdrew to the northwest as pre-ordered.

Meanwhile, Captain Roy's Construction Battalion suffered losses from air attack as it retreated. It soon found itself halfway between American and Soviet spearheads about 20km away. American tanks caused them further deaths just as the battalion was dispersing, and another group was surprised by a Russian vanguard, again sustaining unforeseen losses.

The remains of the 5th Company, about sixty men, reached the southern end of Schwerin town, which is bordered to the east by Schwerinsee Lake, from which a canal runs to the south. The town was already occupied by the Americans holding the western edge of the lake, while Soviet troops bordered the east side of the canal. With their backs to the canal, the company used up the last of its cartridges against the Soviets, while its left flank made contact with the Americans, to whom they then surrendered.

As a result of the Soviet advance in Pomerania, the *Charlemagne*'s Training and Replacement Battalion under SS-Lieutenant-Colonel Hersche had moved from Greifenberg to Wildflecken, where other elements of the Division congregated, amounting to a force of 1,200 men. Hersche organised them into a March Battalion under SS-Major Katzian of 3 combat companies, a 400-strong Special Battalion under SS-Major von Lölhöffel consisting of 2 construction companies and a penal company, and a transport unit and workshop company under Lieutenant Maudhuit.

On 18 March, *Reichsführer-SS* Heinrich Himmler ordered the March Battalion to rejoin the Division. The battalion set off on foot on the night of 30/31 March for Neustrelitz with American forces less than 20km away. Marching day and night and keeping away from the main roads subjected to air attack, the battalion barely managed to keep ahead of the American advance. By 13 April the column was beginning to disintegrate and men were deserting when SS-Lieutenant-General Berger from the Main Security Office addressed the troops and announced that they were not going to Mecklenburg but to Bavaria, to the 'Mountain Redoubt' where the Reich would conduct a last-ditch stand. The last 600 men were taken by train to Regensburg on the Danube, where they split into 2 with some of the men being attached to the 38th SS-Grenadier Division *Nibelungen*.

The remainder continued marching south. On the 18th they fought a delaying action near Wartenberg, but were swept aside. Eleven days later, now re-equipped, they fought another action in defence of a bridge over the Amper River, and on the next day, the 30th, a further action in defence of a bridge over the Isar. The unit then disintegrated, the men going their separate ways. It was some of these men that were taken prisoner by the Americans near Bad Reichenhalle, only to be handed over to General Leclerk's 2nd Armoured Division when the Americans moved on.

The subsequent fate of survivors of the *Charlemagne* varied considerably. A few escaped to South America and eventually died under circumstances that appear to have been engineered by French *Deuxième Bureau* agents. A few escaped Soviet or Allied captivity, while others eventually returned to France only to be imprisoned or executed after trial.

Annex A

The Formation of a French Regiment
of the Waffen-SS

Communiqué issued at a press conference in Paris on 6 August 1943.

With the law of 22 July 1943, President Laval, with the assent of the Head of State, Marshal Pétain, recognises the right of all Frenchmen to enlist in the formations of the Waffen-SS in the east in order to participate in the fighting for the existence and future of Europe.

By virtue of this law, the volunteers for the Waffen-SS enjoy the same legal status as members of the LVF.

The French Government has thus shown that it appreciates the offer made by the Führer and that it is ready to play its part in the obligations demanded at this decisive time in the fate of Europe.

It is clear that the formation of a unit of French volunteers within the body of the Waffen-SS represents a new and very important step in the unification of European youth against bolchevist nihilism.

The fact is that through the influx of volunteers from almost all the European countries, who, side by side with their German comrades, are distinguishing themselves by their valour on the Eastern Front, the SS, essential fundament of the National Socialist Party that since its beginning only had an internal

German political value, has become transformed today into an indissoluble community of European youth fighting for the maintenance of its cultural values and civilisation.

That French youth has reacted instinctively to this new step is demonstrated by the fact that within several days, and with hardly any propaganda, more than 1,500 volunteers have come forward. The first battalion exists and soon the first French SS regiment will be in the course of proving the permanence of the high French military tradition and the combatant spirit of its youngsters.

The SS will make itself a point of honour and will consider it an essential task of using the military qualities and will to fight of every Frenchman disposed to engage his life in the fight for the existence and future of Europe against Bolchevism for social justice – for victory!

Conditions of Engagement
Except for Jews and those with a criminal conviction, all Frenchmen, bachelors or married men, normally developed and suitable for military training, may enlist in the Waffen-SS.
Age 17–40; Height 1.65m.

Conditions of Promotion in the Waffen-SS
Those volunteers, simple soldiers at the time of enlistment, that show the required aptitude, can be admitted to the officer and NCO schools of the Waffen-SS. Admittance to these schools will not be determined by the candidates' diplomas or university degrees, but solely by their proven personal qualities and aptitude for command.

Command will be Exercised Jointly by German and French Officers
French officers and NCOs will have the opportunity of regaining their ranks and receiving commands after attending a course at the

Waffen–SS officer and NCO schools. The courses will include instruction and examination in capacity and aptitude for command.

In addition, those simple soldier volunteers showing the required aptitudes could also be admitted to the same schools.

The General Situation for French Volunteers
Basically no difference is made between volunteers in the Waffen–SS, they all undergo the German Waffen-SS regime.

The Waffen–SS being the big family of the new Europe's young combatants, the French volunteers will have exactly the same duties and obligations, but also the same advantages, as their German, Nowegian, Danish, Dutch, Fleming, Walloon or Swiss comrades.

The Initial Command Structures

Inspectorate of French SS Units
Inspector: SS–Maj-Gen Dr Gustav Krukenberg

ADCs	SS-2/Lt Valentin Patzak	Liaison Offrs	SS-Lt Kurt Dally
	SS-2/Lt Hegewald		SS-2/Lt Heinz Gehring
Ia (Operations)	SS-Capt Hans-Robert Jauss	Gd & Trg Coy	SS-Lt Wilhelm Weber
Ib (QM)	SS-Lt Meier	Gendarmerie	SS-Lt Görr
Ic (Int)	SS-Capt Dr Julius Schmidt		
IIa/b (Personnel)	SS-Capt Paul Pachur		
IVa (Intendant)	SS-Capt Karl-Heinz Hagen	Chief Instructor	SS-Col Walter Zimmermann
Admin	SS-Capt Gewecke	Bde Liaison	Capt Jean-Michel Renault
	SS-Capt Wilhelm Reinholdt	Passive Defence	SS-Maj Katzian
	SS-Lt Harald Wahrlich	Others	SS-2/Lt Ernst Friedrich
IVb (Medical)	SS-Maj Dr Wolfgang Schlegel		SS-2/Lt Alfred Zander
Ivc (Vet)	SS-Capt Dr Artur Scheiner		SS-2/Lt Gerd Engel
V (Transport)	SS-2/Lt Gustav-Adolf Neubauer		
VI (Political)	SS-Lt Dr Erich Kopp		

HQ Brigade Charlemagne
Comd: Brig Edgar Joseph Puaud

Ia & COS	Major Jean de Vaugelas		
ADCs	Lt Michel Auphan	Hon Members	Maj Jacques Doriot
	O/Cdt Betrand Platon		Maj Joseph Darnand
Ic (Int)	Lt Jacques Delile	Detached	Lt-Col Paul Gamory-Dubourdeau
IIa/b (personnel)	Lt Maurice Bénétoux	- SS Main Office	
IVb (Medical)	Lt Dr Marc Lelongt	- Neweklau	Lt Cance
IVc (Vet)	Capt Dr Jean Richert	- Neweklau	2/Lt Kreis
IVd (Chaplains)	Lt Jean de Mayol de Lupé (later) 2/Lt Just Verney	Liaison (Insp)	SS-Lt Erich von Lölhöffel (later) SS-Maj Roemheld
VI (Political)	SS-2/Lt Dr Heinrich Bueler	Passive Defence	Lt Multrier
		Gendarmerie	Lt Veyrieras

HQ Coy	Sgt-Maj Surrel	Workshop Coy	Lt Henri Maud'huit
Signals Coy	Lt Jean-Auguste Dupuyau	Construction Coy	Lt de Moroge
Engineer Coy	Lt Roger Audibert de Vitrolles	Medical Coy	Lt Dr Bonnefoy
Veterinary Coy	Lt Dr Richter	Supply Column A	Lt Schisler
		Supply Column B	Lt Croisille

Waffen-Grenadier Regiment der SS 57 (frz. 1)
Comd: Maj Victor de Bourmont

Adjt	2/Lt Jean Artus		
Liaison Offr	2/Lt Christian Martres		
Reserve	Lt de Londaize		
II (Personnel)	2/Lt Jean-Marie Stehli	HQ Coy	Lt André
IVb (Medical)	Capt Dr Eugène Leproux	A/Tk Coy	Lt Labuz
IVv (Vet)	Lt Dr Jean Vergniaud	Inf Gun Coy	Capt Robert
1st Battalion		**2nd Battalion**	
Comd	Lt Henri Fenet	Comd	Capt René Obitz
Adjt	2/Lt Pierre Hug	Adjt	
Liaison Offr	O/Cdt Jean Labourdette	Liaison Offr	
Med Offr	SS-O/Cdt Ludwig Anneshaensel SS-O/Cdt Siedow	Med Off	Lt Dr Marcel Herpe
No. 1 Coy	2/Lt Jacques Brazier	No. 5 Coy	Lt Lucien Hennecart
No. 2 Coy	Lt Ivan Bartolomei	No. 6 Coy	2/Lt Pierre Albert
No. 3 Coy	2/Lt Guy Counil	No. 7 Coy	O/Cdt Million-Rousseau
No. 4 Coy	Lt Couvreur	No. 8 Coy	2/Lt Phillipe Colnion

Waffen-Grenadier Regiment der SS 58 (frz. 2)
Comd: Maj Emile Raybaud

Adjt	Lt Baudouin		
Liaison Offr	O/Cdt Victor de Vaugelas		
II (personnel)	Capt Justin Jotard	HQ Coy	Capt de Perricot
IVb (Medical)	Lt Dr Pierre Métais	A/Tk Coy	Sgt-Maj Robert Girard
	SS-2/Lt Goliberzuch	Inf Gun Coy	Lt François

1st Battalion		**2nd Battalion**	
Comd	Capt Monneuse	Comd	Capt Maurice Berrier
Adjt	Sgt-Maj Caténés	Adjt	2/Lt Michel du Verdier
Liaision Offr	O/Cdt Jean Chatrousse	Med Offr	2/Lt Dr Joubert
Med Offr	2/Lt Dr Thibaud		
No. 1 Coy	Lt Pierre Fatin	No. 5 Coy	Sgt-Maj Walter
No. 2 Coy	Lt Géromini	No. 6 Coy	Lt Michel Saint Magne
No. 3 Coy	2/Lt Yves Rigeade	No. 7 Coy	Lt Georges Wagner
No. 4 Coy	Lt Tardan	No. 8 Coy	Lt Paul Defever

SS-Artillery Battalion 57

Comd	Capt Havette	Comd	Jacques Martin
Adjt	Capt Martin	Adjt	O/Cdt Mast
		Ranging Offr	Lt Chauffour
		Supply Column	Sgt-Maj Marméjean
Vet	2/Lt Dr René Fraysse		

1st Bty Lt Chillou 2nd Bty Lt Louis Salle   3rd Bty O/Cdt Henri Le Guichaoua

SS-Tank-Hunting Battalion 57

Comd	Maj Jean Boudet-Gheusi	Flak Bty	2/Lt Jean Fayard
Liaison	O/Cdt Georges Radici	Hy A/Tk Coy	O/Cdt Vinçenot
	O/Cdt Serge Krotoff	SPG Coy	Lt Pierre Michel
Intendant	SS-Lt Weiss	SPG Escort Coy	Sgt-Maj Mongourd
Medical	Lt Dr Durandy		
Div Liaision	SS-Capt Kroepsch		

SS-Field Replacement Battalion

Comd	Capt Biaud
Adjt	SS-Lt Ludwig
1st March Coy	2/Lt Paul Pignard-Berthet
2nd March Coy	Capt Flamand
3rd March Coy	Lt de Brégaud

SS-Training and Replacement Battalion
(Greifenberg)

Comd	SS-Lt Heinrich Hersche
Judge-Advocate	SS-Lt Dick
Depot Coy	SS-Lt Allgeier
Recruit Coy	Lt Pierre Crespin
Training Coy	SS-Lt Schüler

Bibliography

Bernage, Georges. *Berlin 1945*, Bayeux: Heimdal, 2005

Dieckert, Major Kurt and General of Infantry Horst Grossmann. *Der Kampf um Ostpreussen*, Stuttgart: Motorbuch Verlag, 1998 (first published 1960)

Duffy, Christopher. *Red Storm on the Reich*, London: Routledge, 1991

Forbes, Robert. *Pour L'Europe – French Volunteers of the Waffen SS*, Trowbridge: Redwood Books, 2000

Jackson, Julian. *France – The Dark Years 1940–1944*, Oxford: Oxford University Press, 2001

Kieser, Egbert. *Danziger Bucht 1945*, Munich: Bechtle Verlag, 1997 (first published 1978)

Mabire, Jean. *La Brigade Frankreich*, Paris: Librairie Arthème Fayard, 1973

Mabire, Jean. *Berlin in Todeskampf (Mourir à Berlin)*, Preussisch Oldendorf: Verlag K.W. Schütz KG, 1977

Mabire, Jean. *La Division Nordland*, Paris: Librairie Arthème Fayard, 1982

Némirovsky, Irène. *Suite Française*, London: Vintage Books, 2007

Pantenius, Hans Jürgen. *Letzte Schlacht an der Ostfront – Von Döberitz bis Danzig 1944/1945*, Hamburg: Verlag E.S. Mittler & Sohn GmbH, 2002

Paxton, Robert O. *Vichy France*, n.p., n.d.

Rocolle, Colonel Pierre. *Götterdämmerung – La Prise de Berlin*, Indo-China: French Military Press, 1954

Schoenbrun, David: *Soldiers of the Night*, London: Robert Hale, 1981

Schön, Heinz. *Die letzten Kriegstage – Ostseehäfen 1945*, Stuttgart: Motorbuch Verlag, 1995

Tiemann, Ralf: *Die Leibstandarte, Vol IV/2 – Opfergang fü Deutschland – Die Leibstandarte in den letzten Monaten*, Coburg: Nation Europa Verlag, 2000

Trigg, Jonathan: *Hitler's Gauls – The History of the 33rd Waffen Division Charlemagne*, Stroud: Spellmount, 2006

Williamson, Gordon: *Waffen-SS Handbook 1933–1945*, Stroud: Sutton, 2003

Index

Armed Forces Index

German Forces
OKW, vii, 6, 8, 13, 96